Welcome to

LIONS
IN
SERENITY

Color Test Page

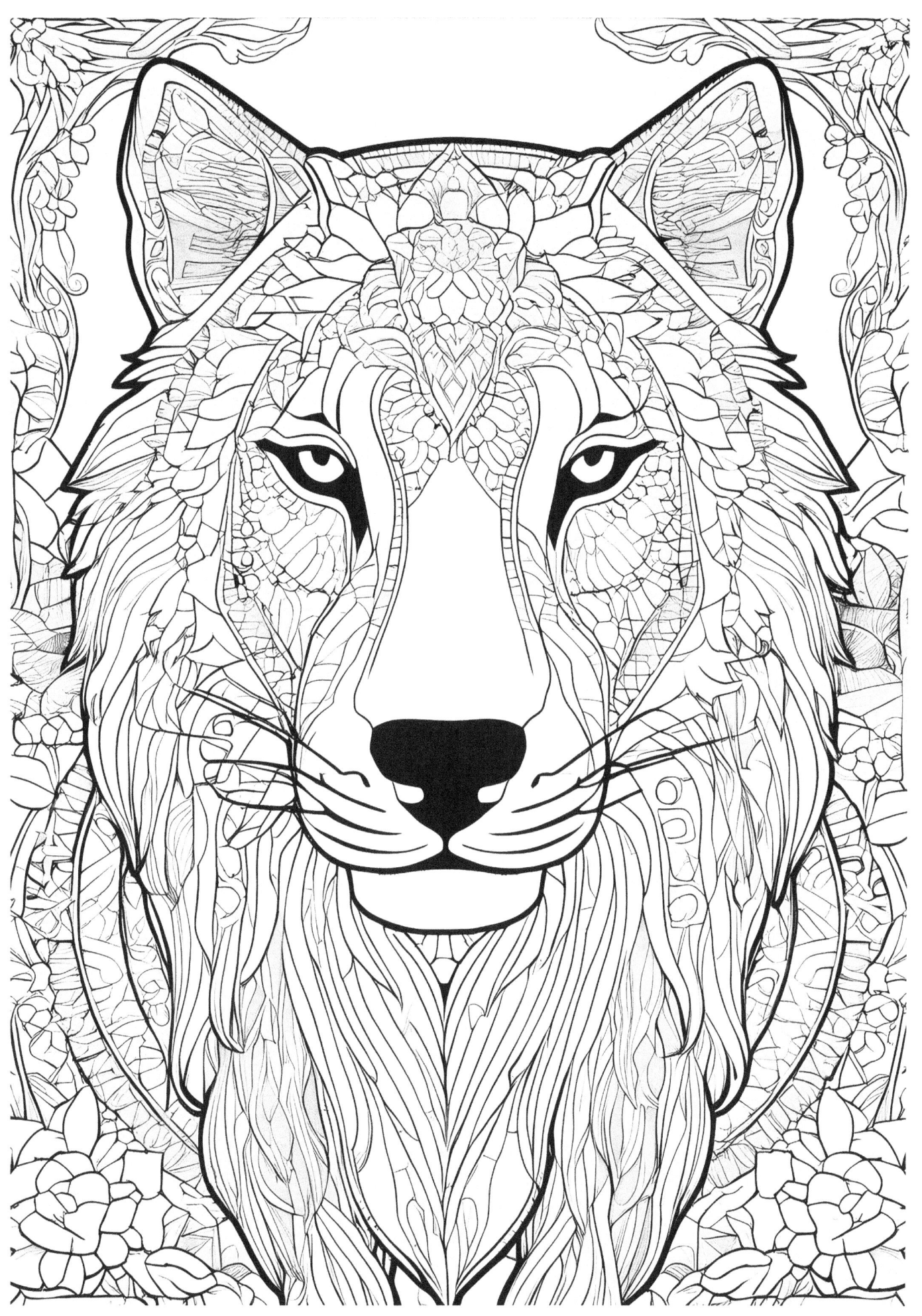

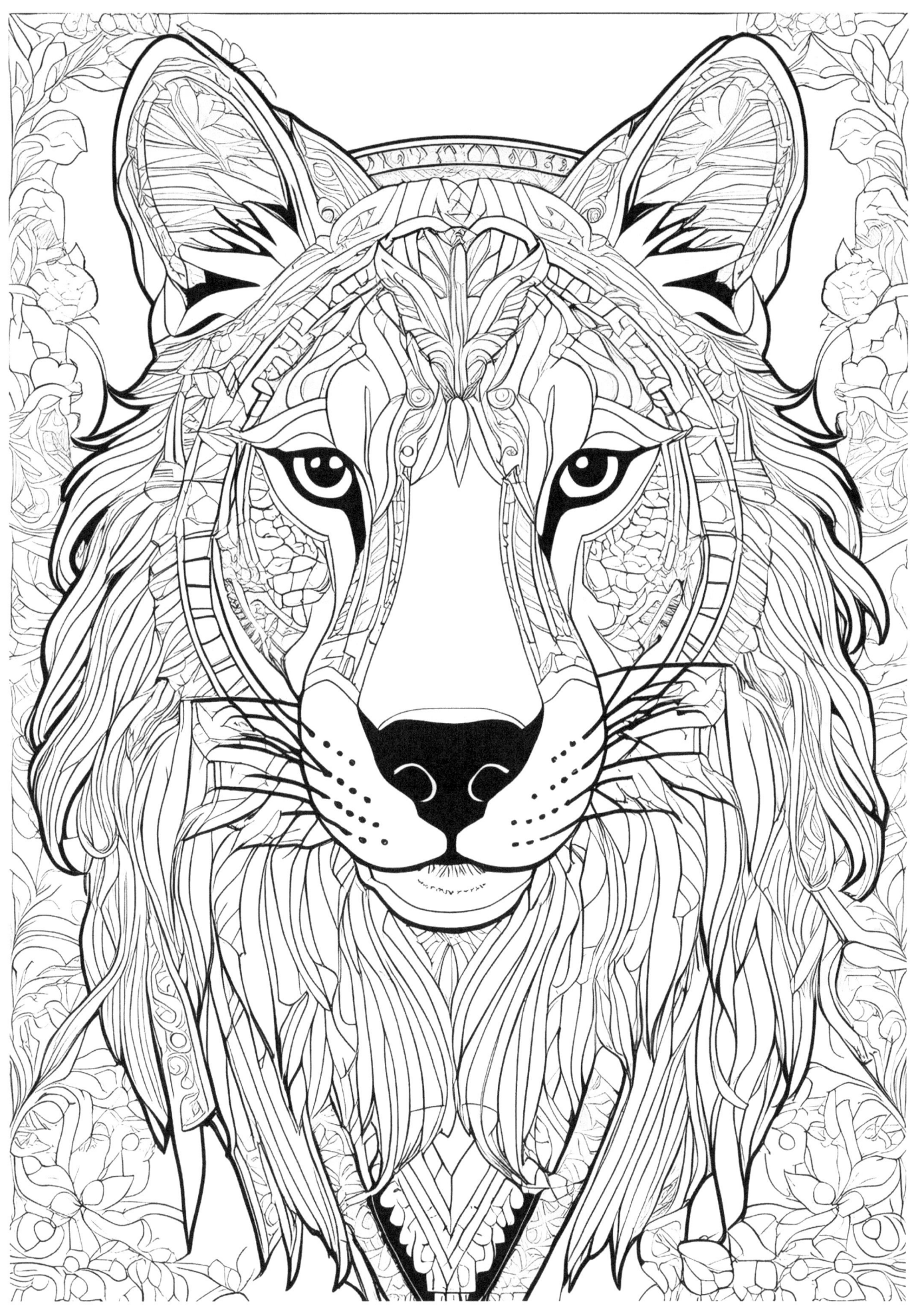

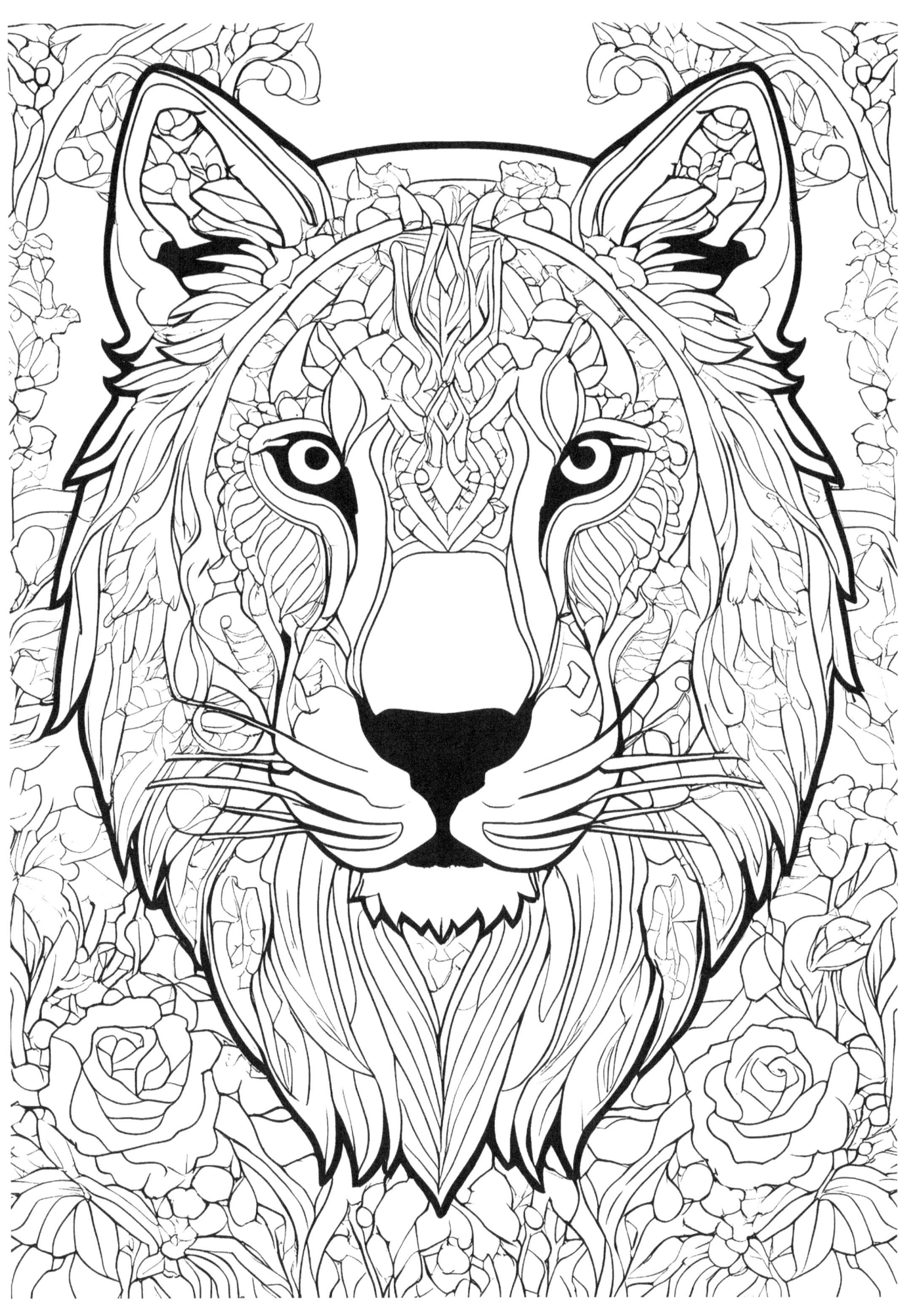

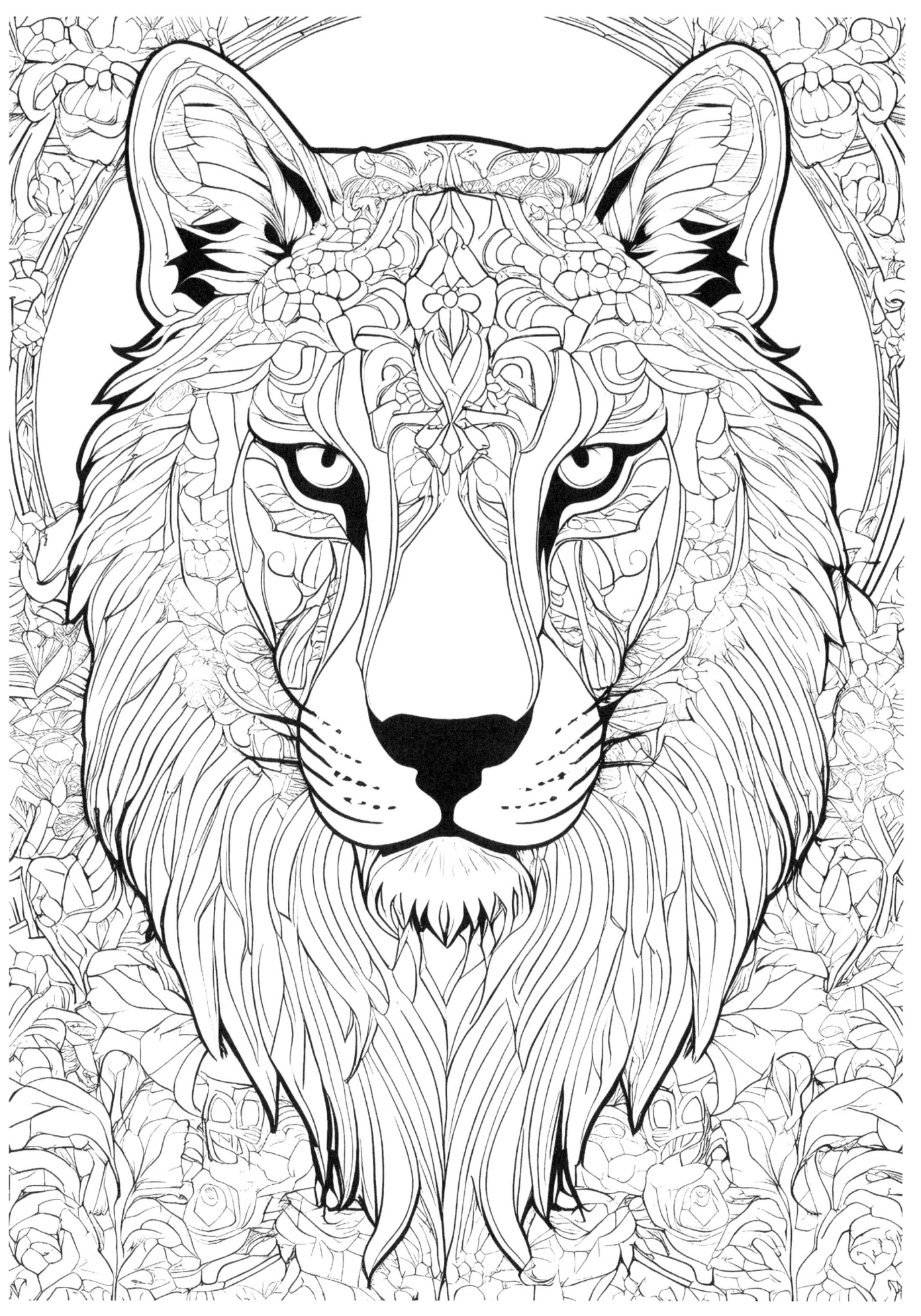

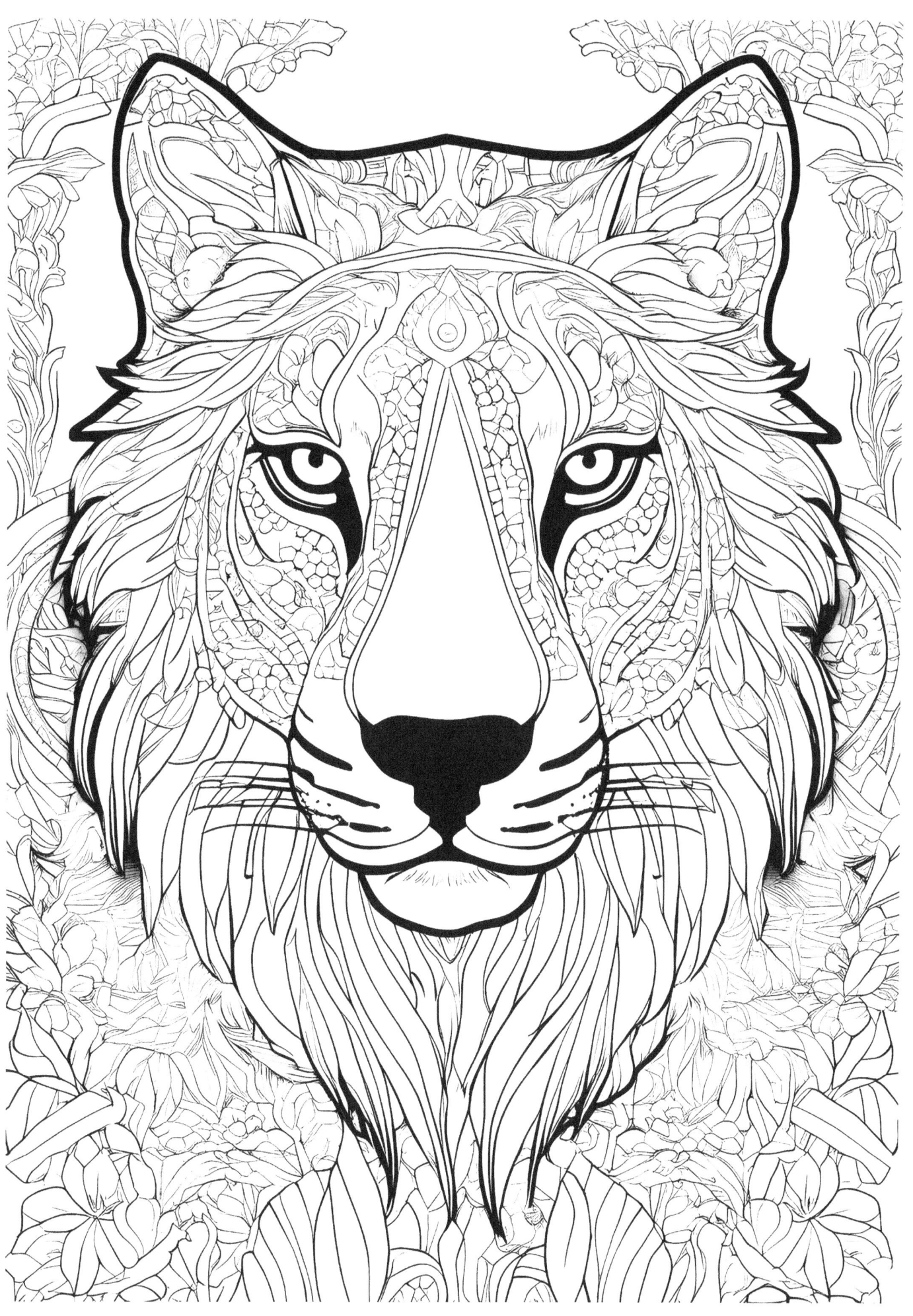

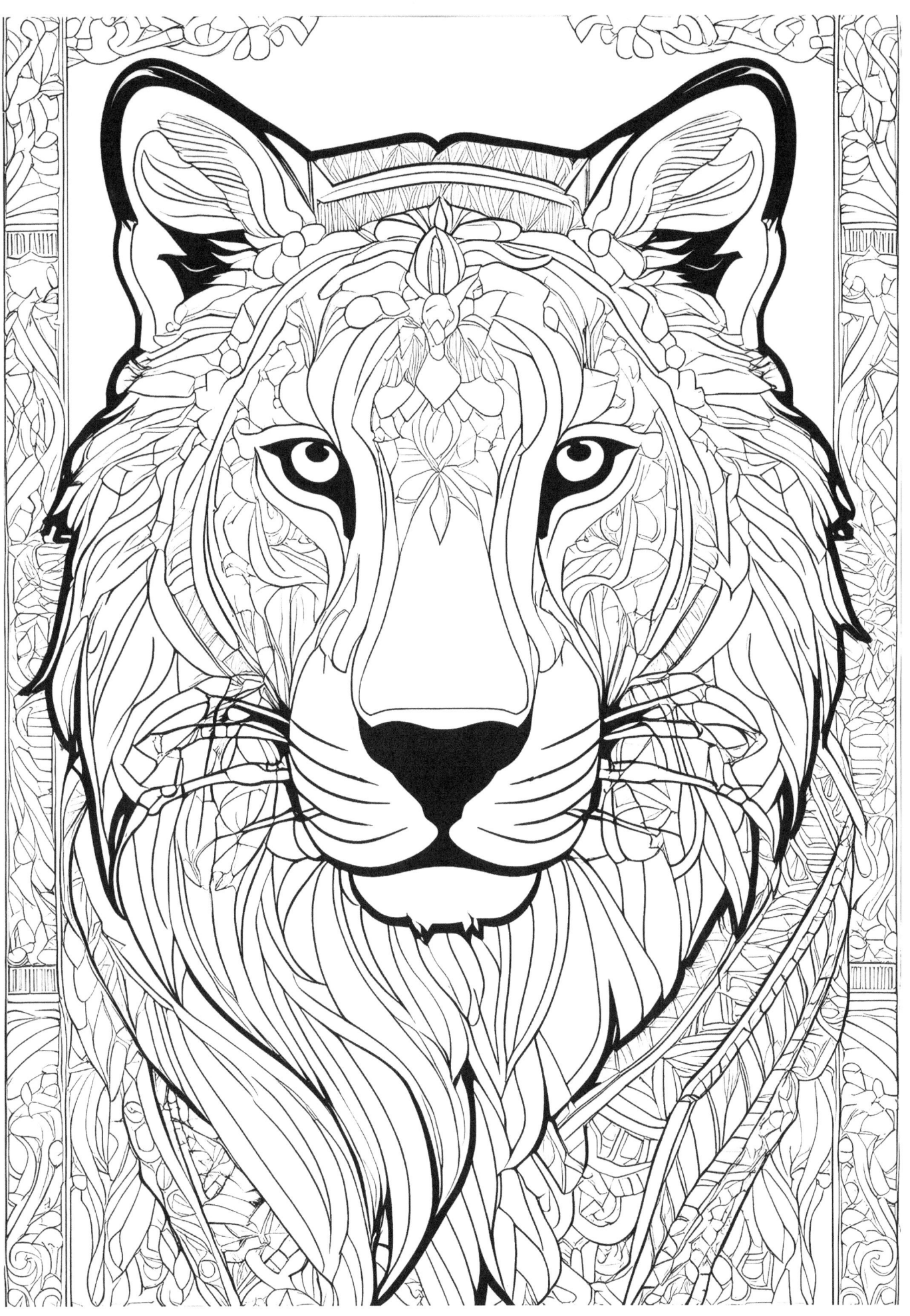

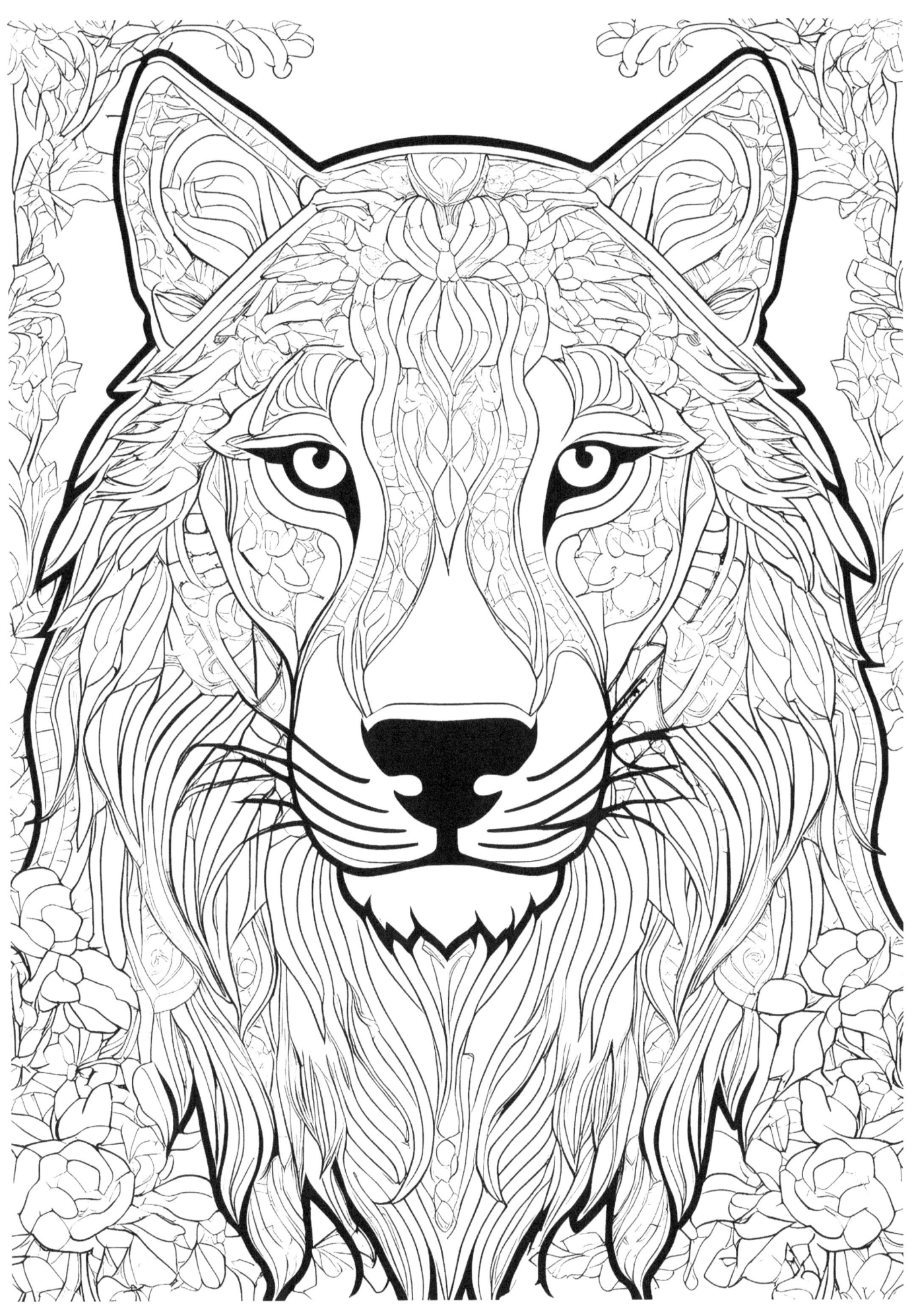

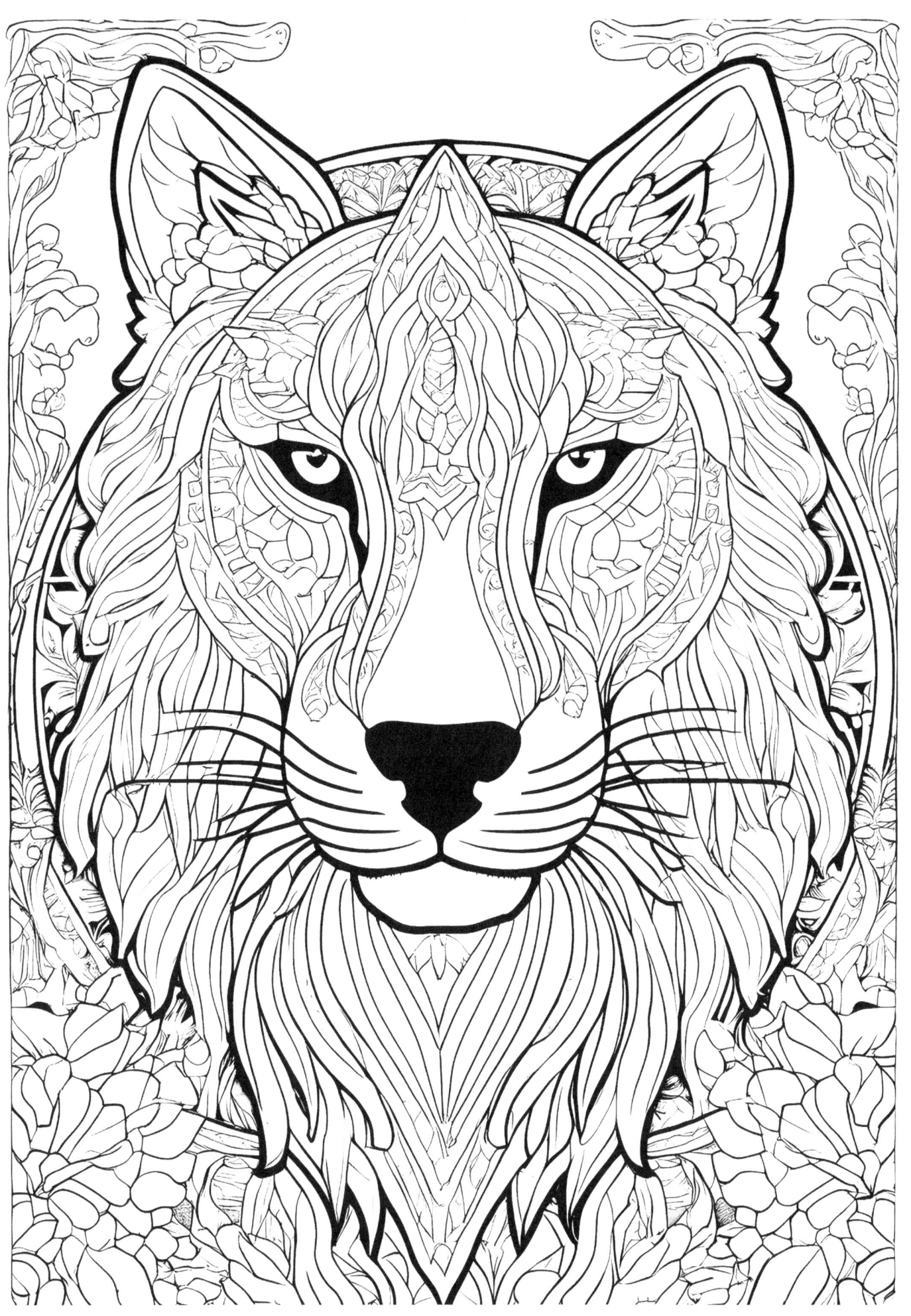

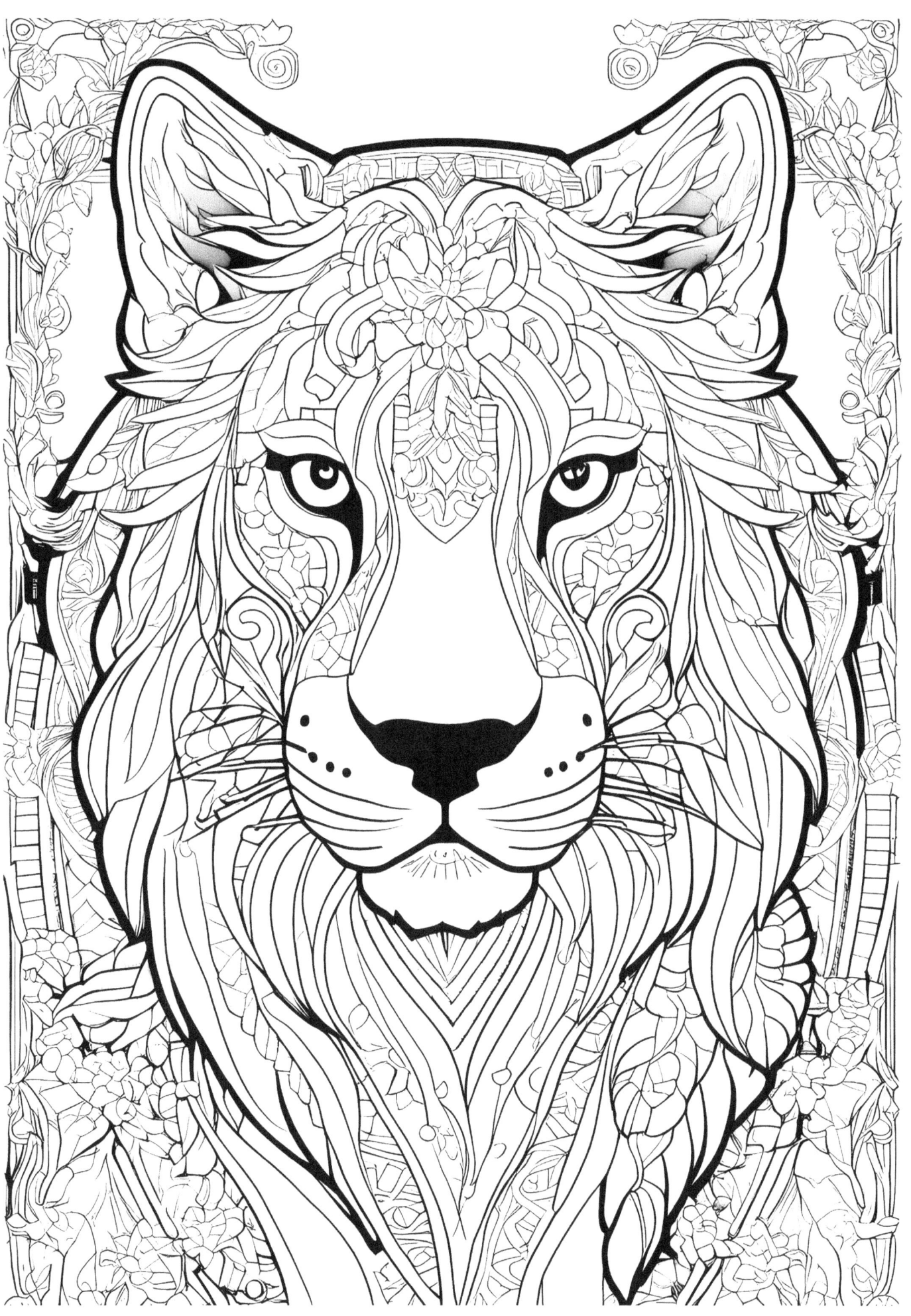

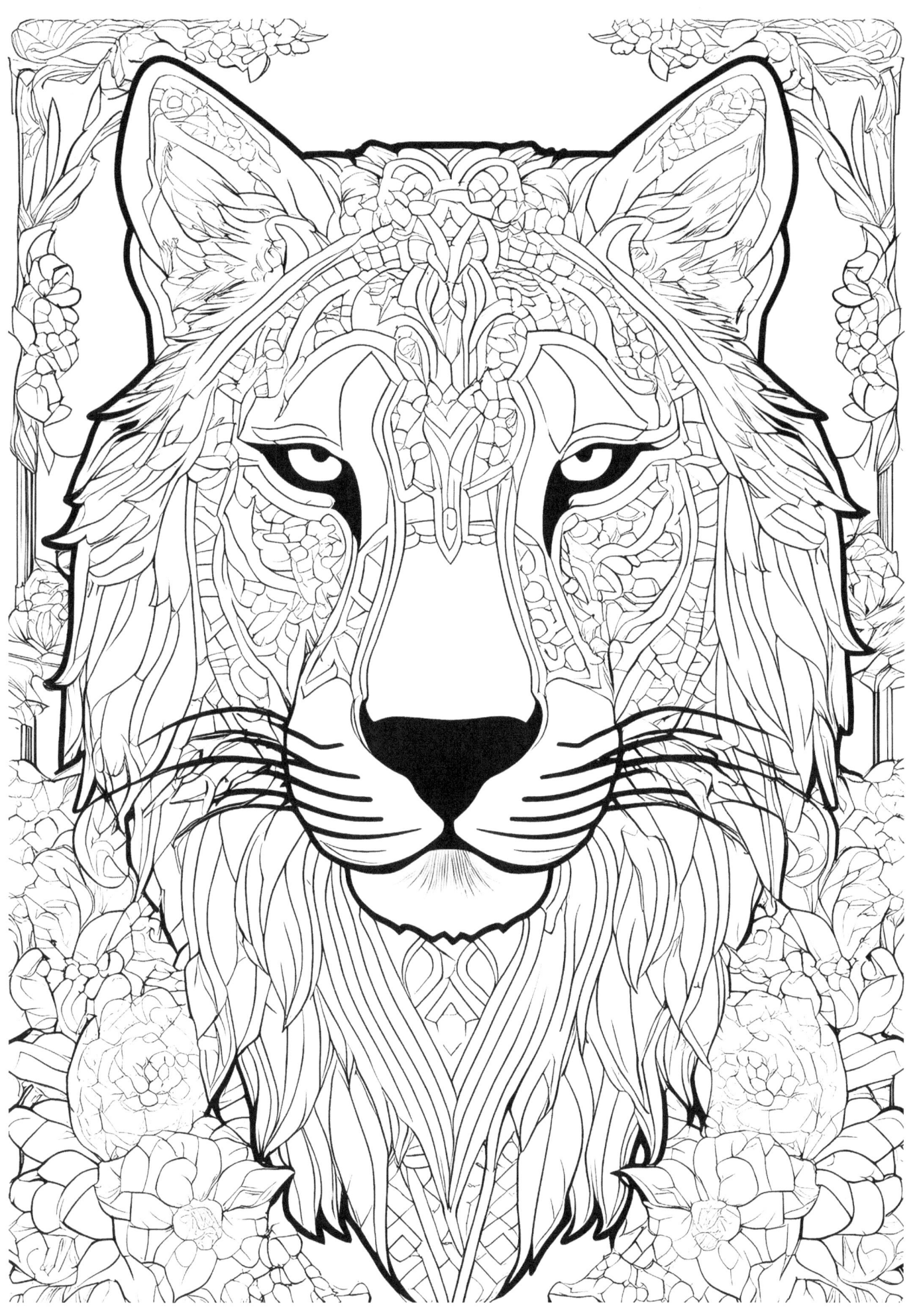

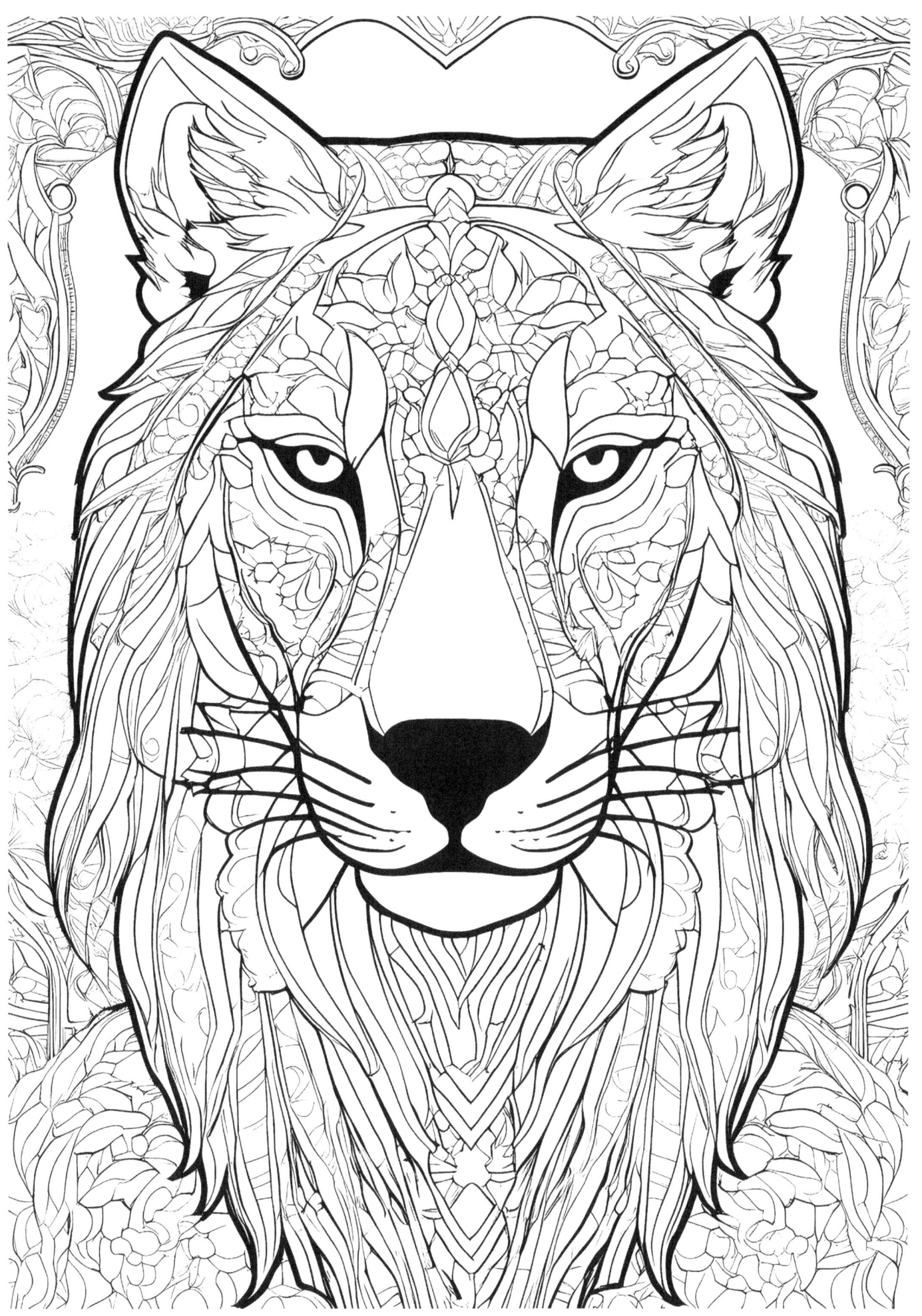

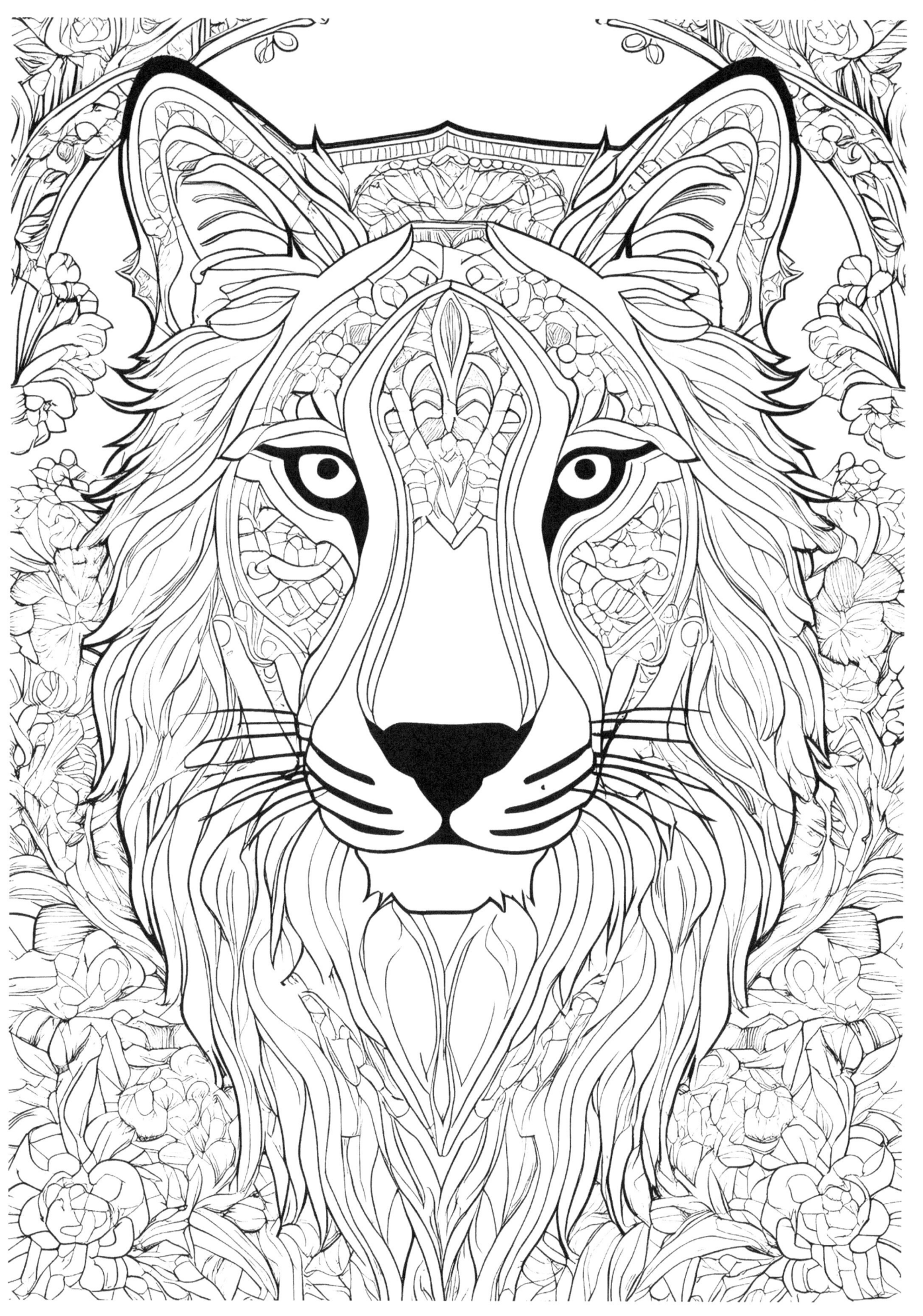

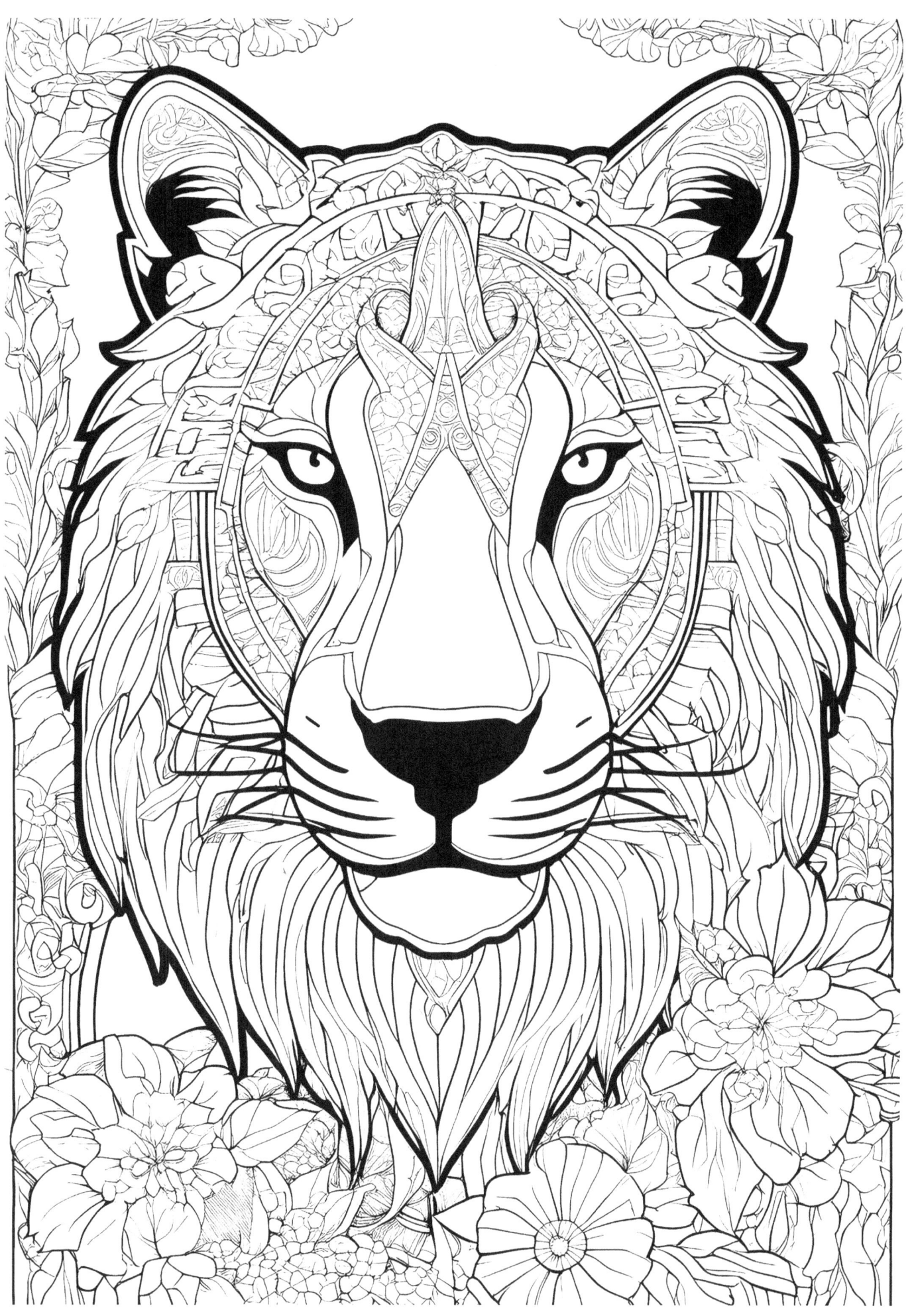

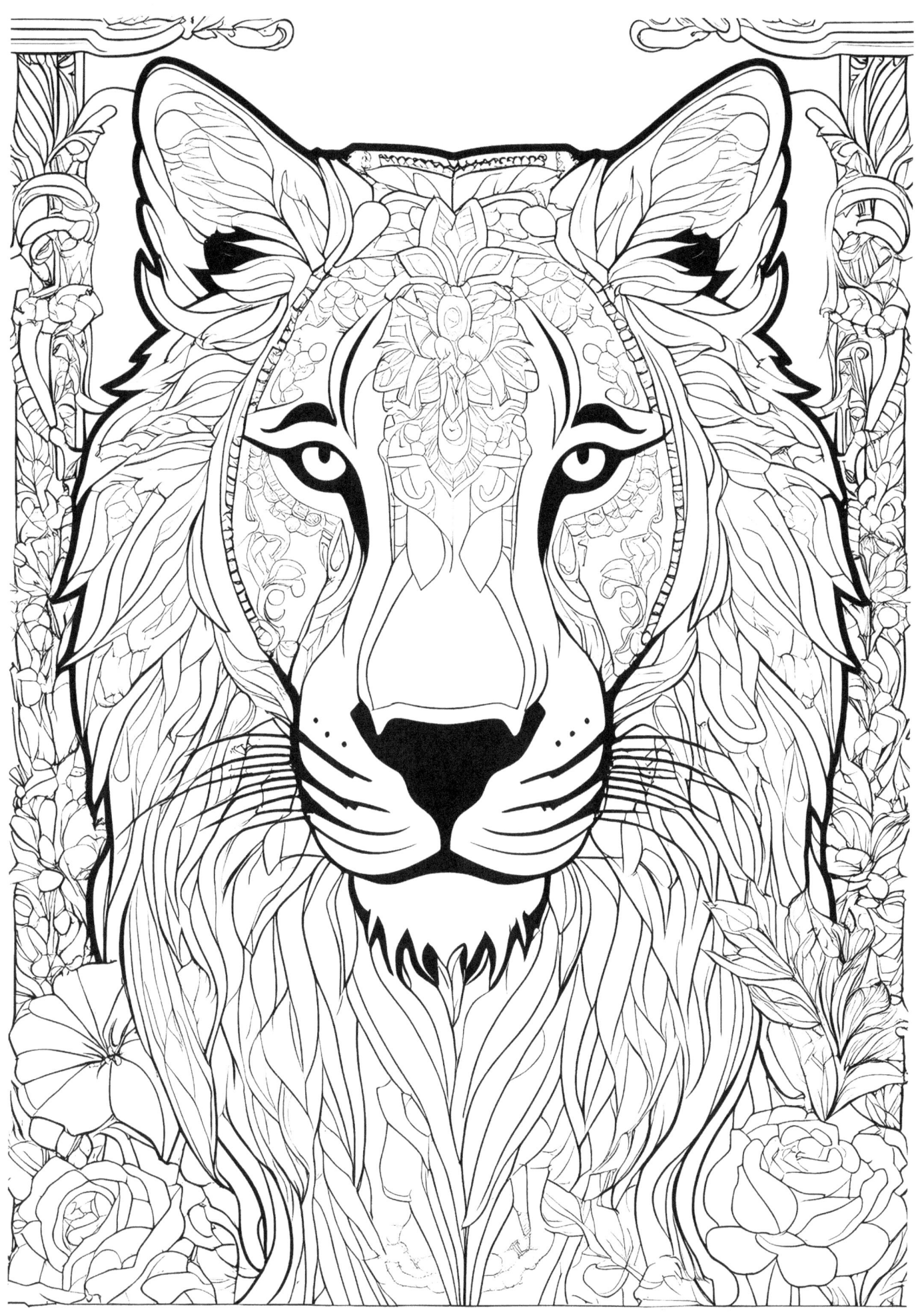

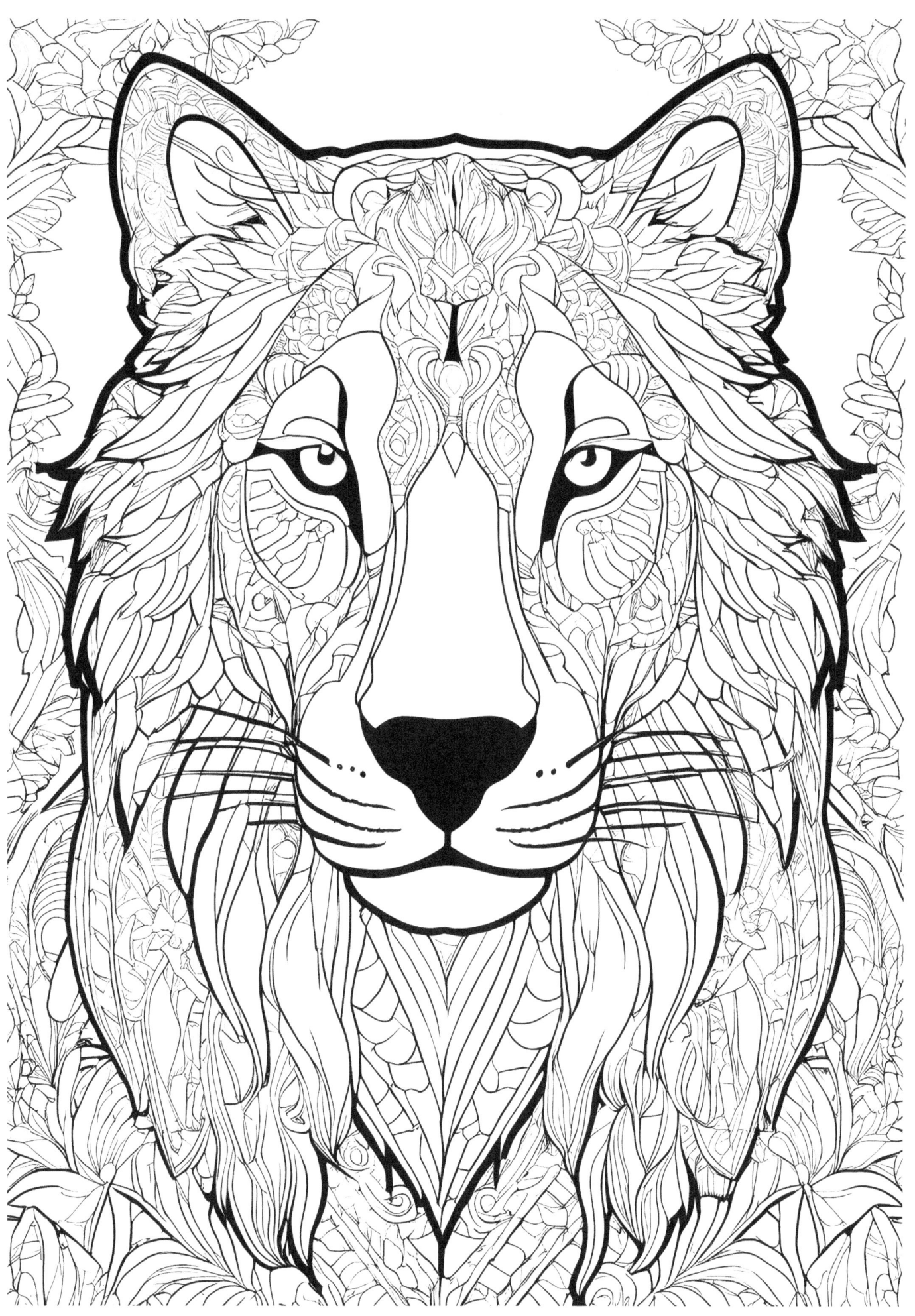

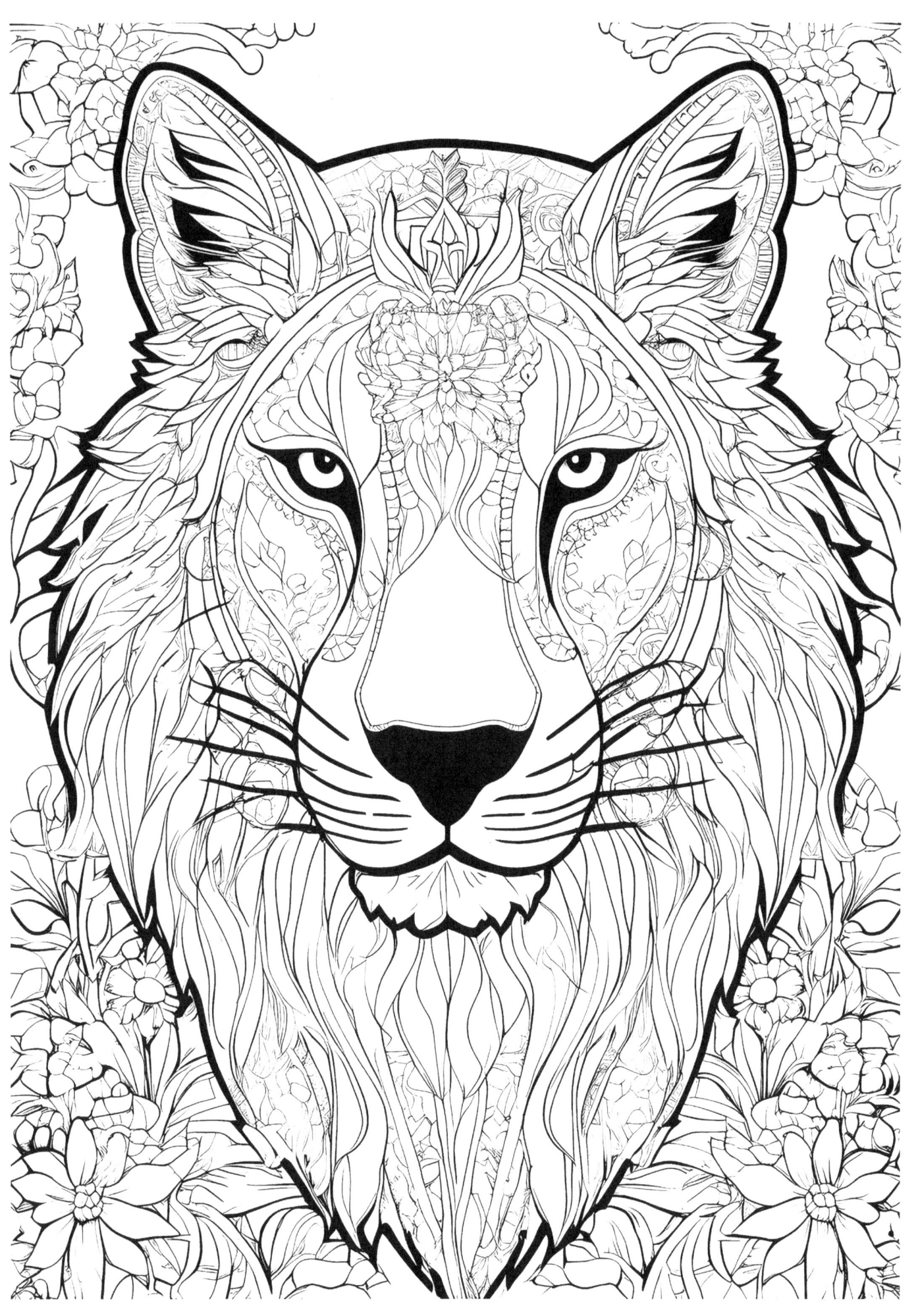

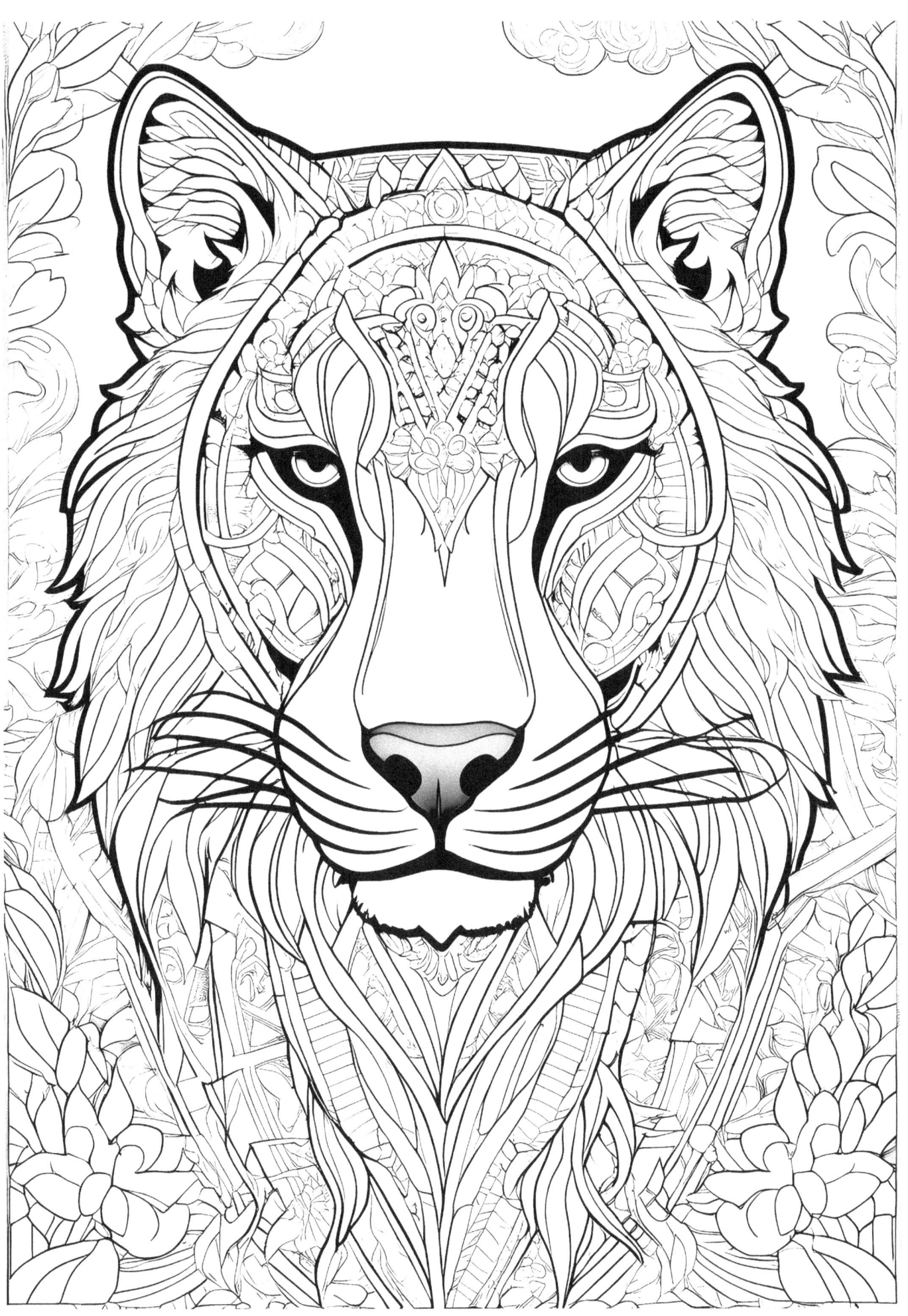

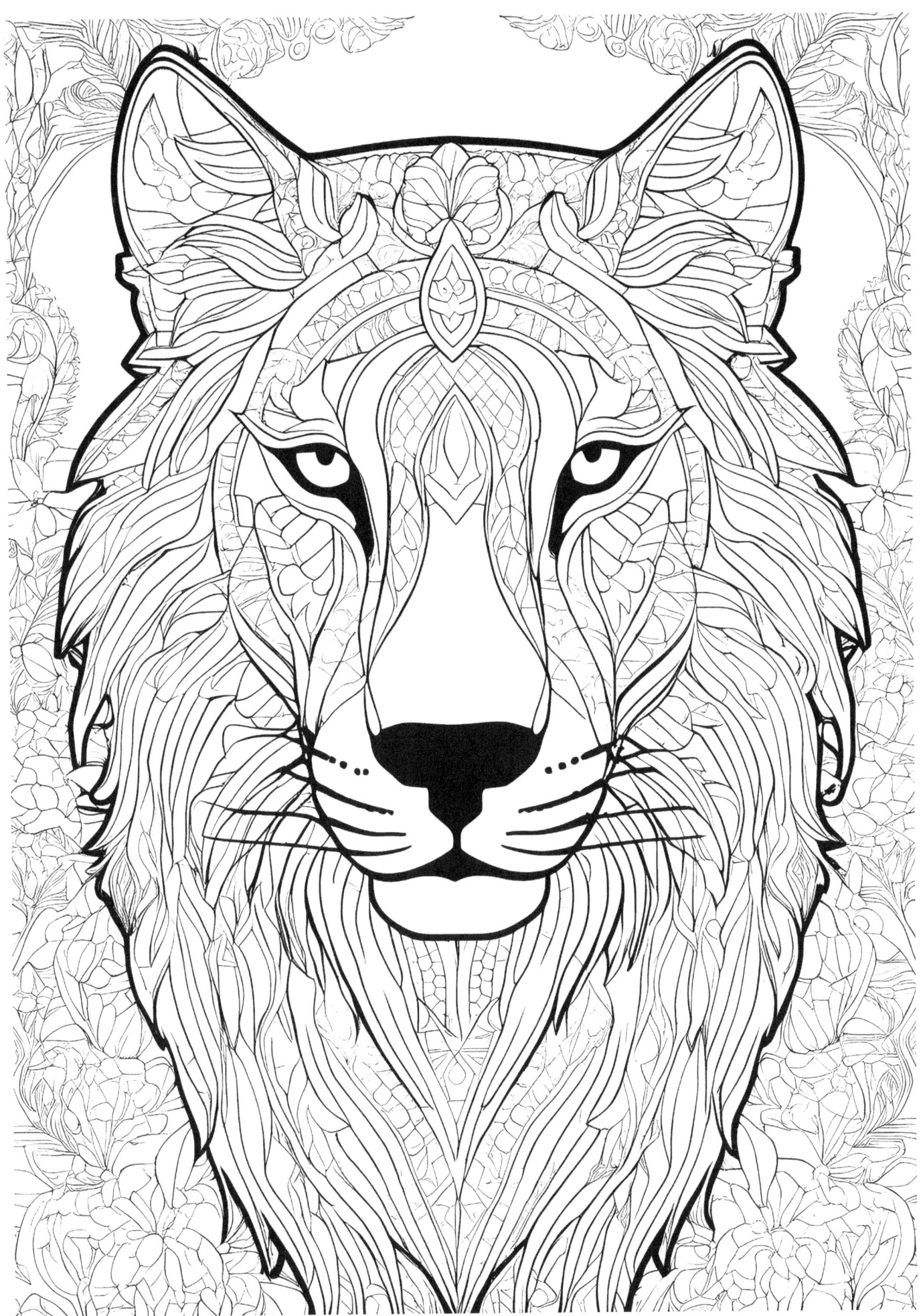

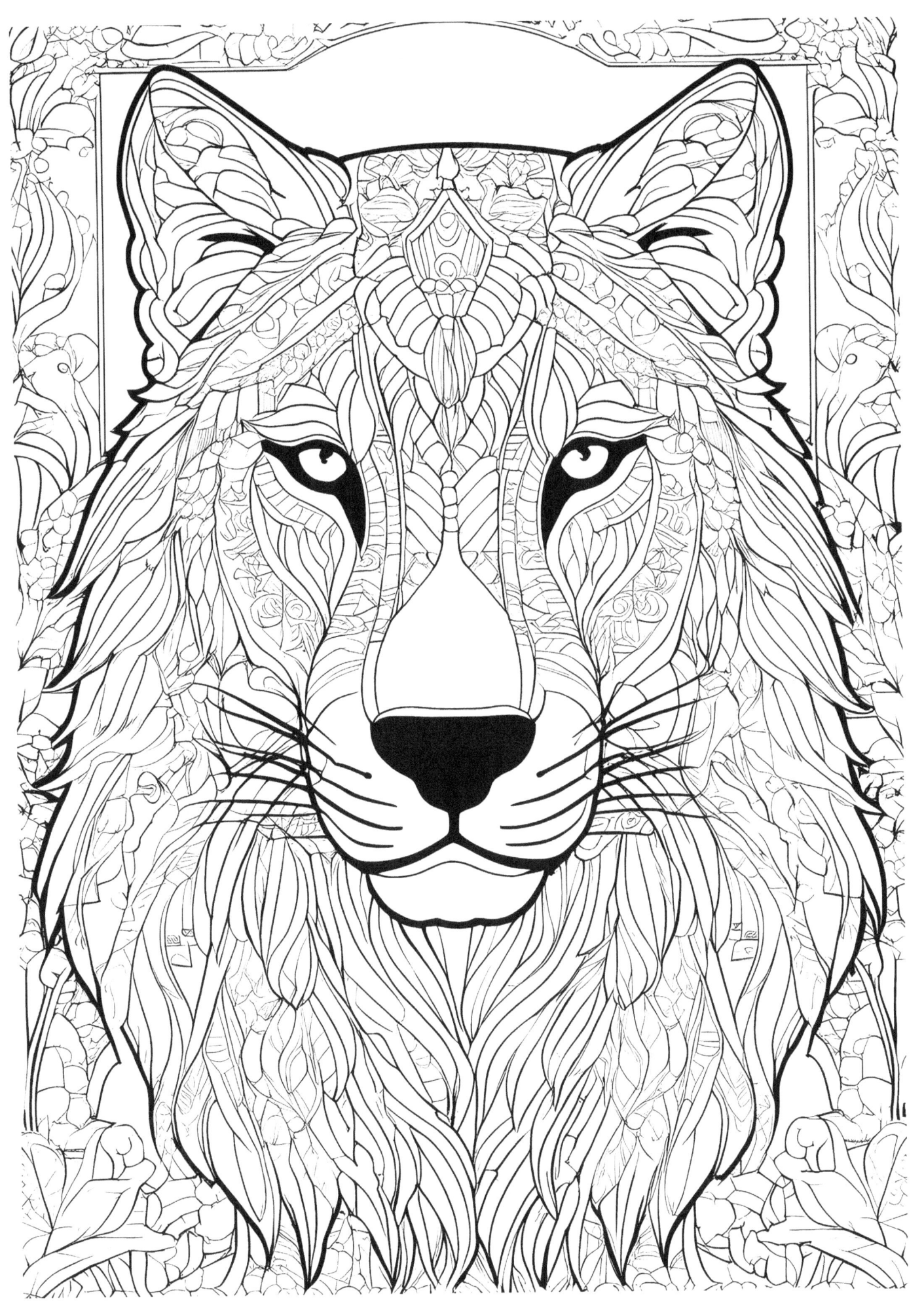

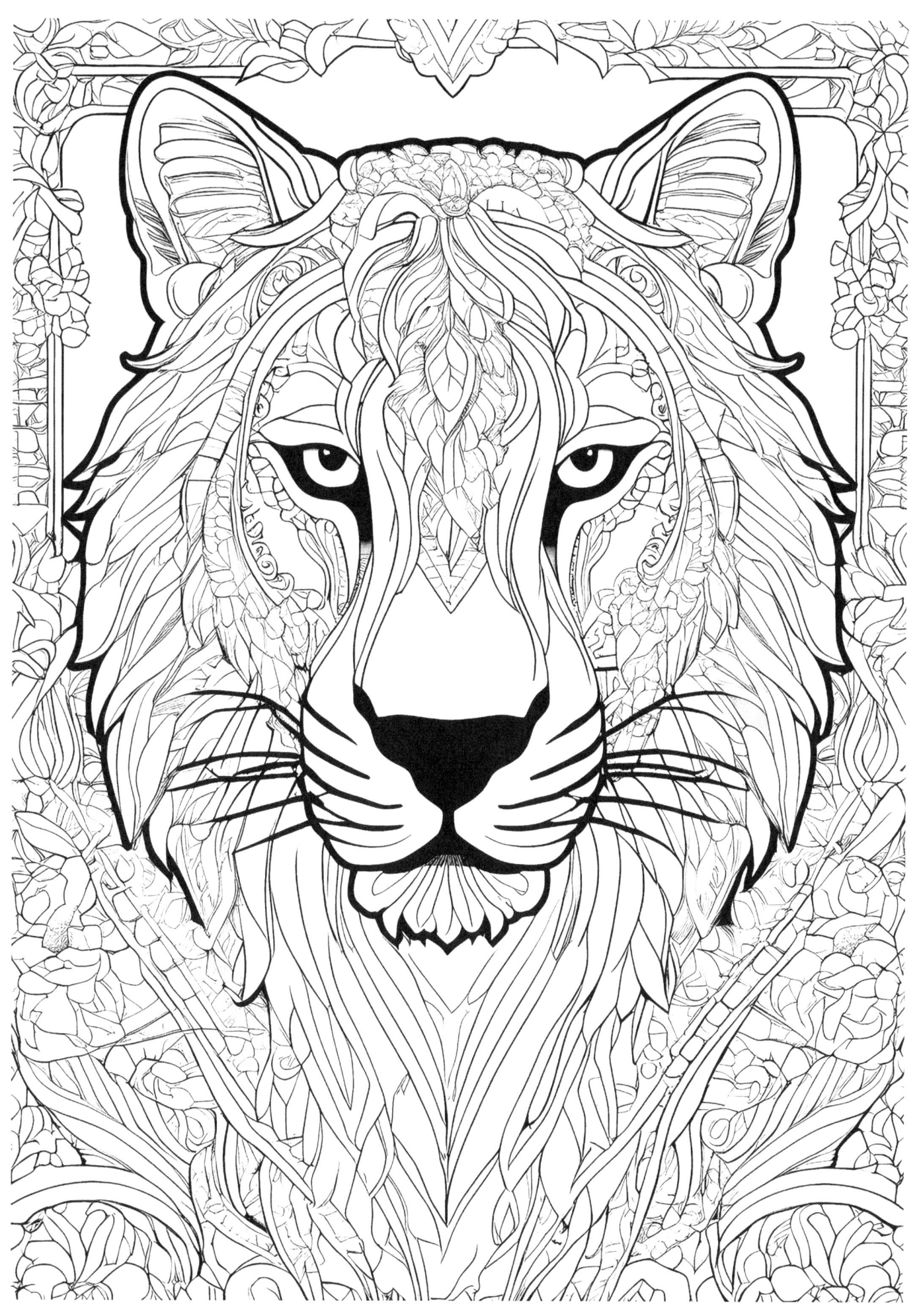

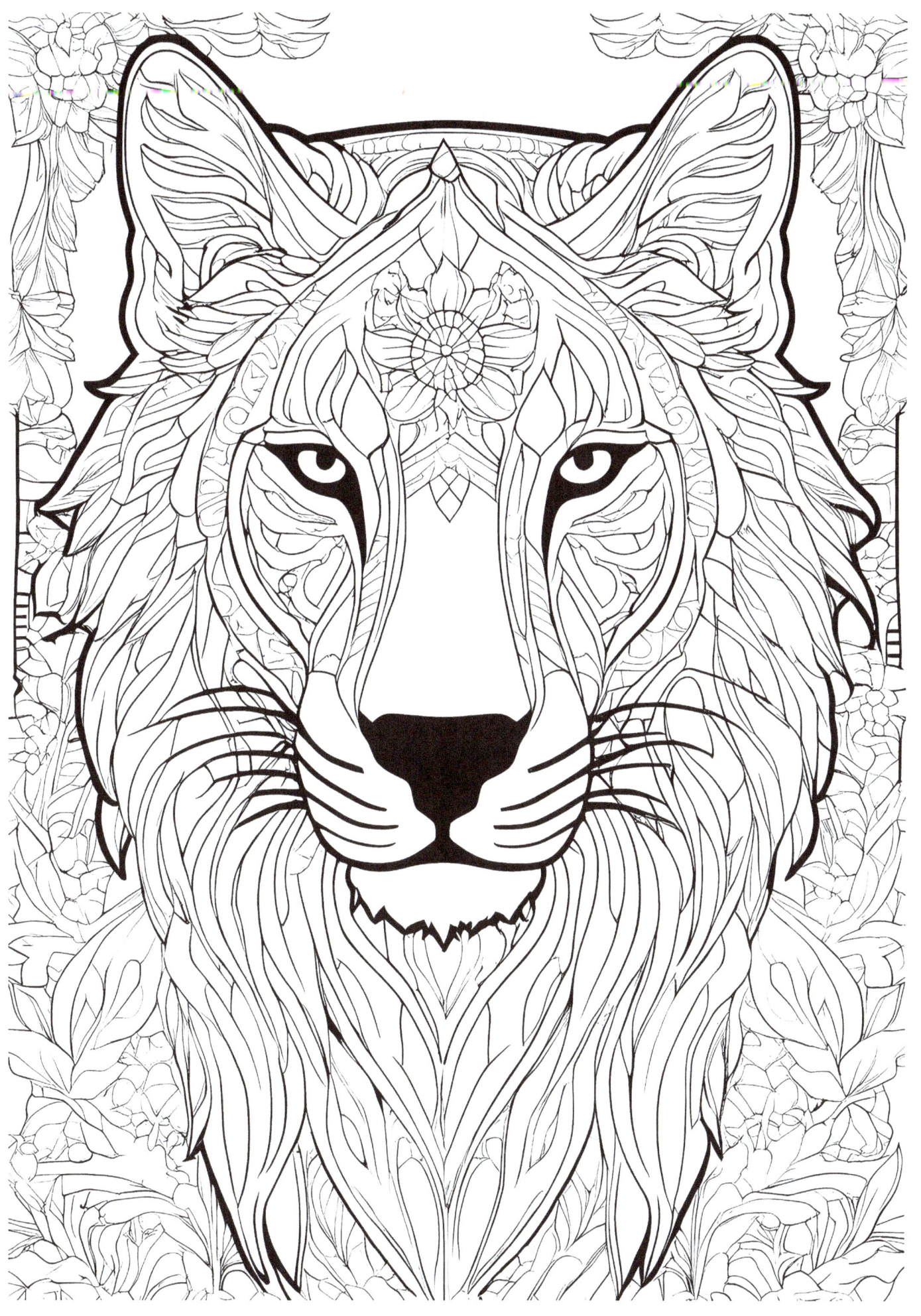

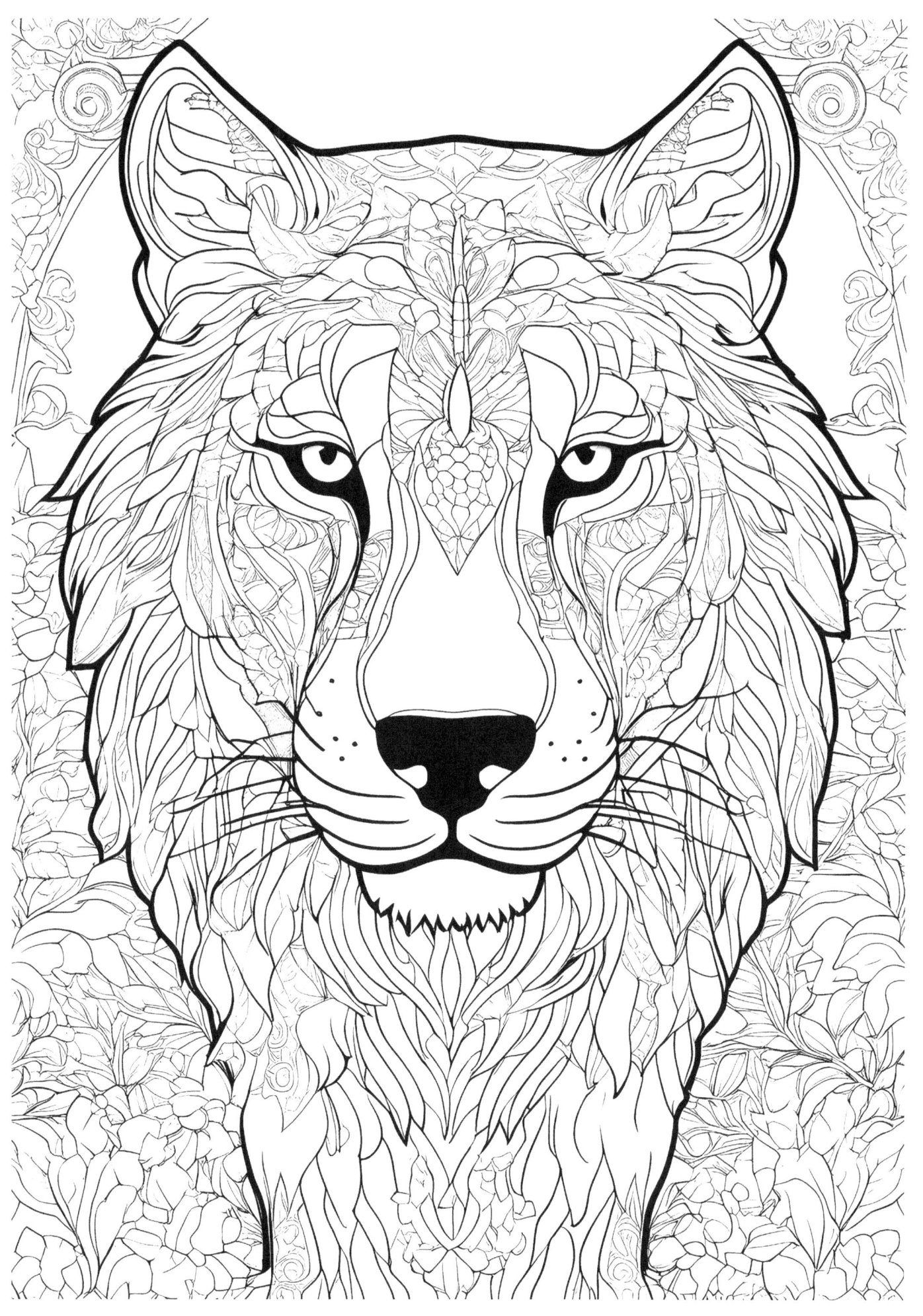

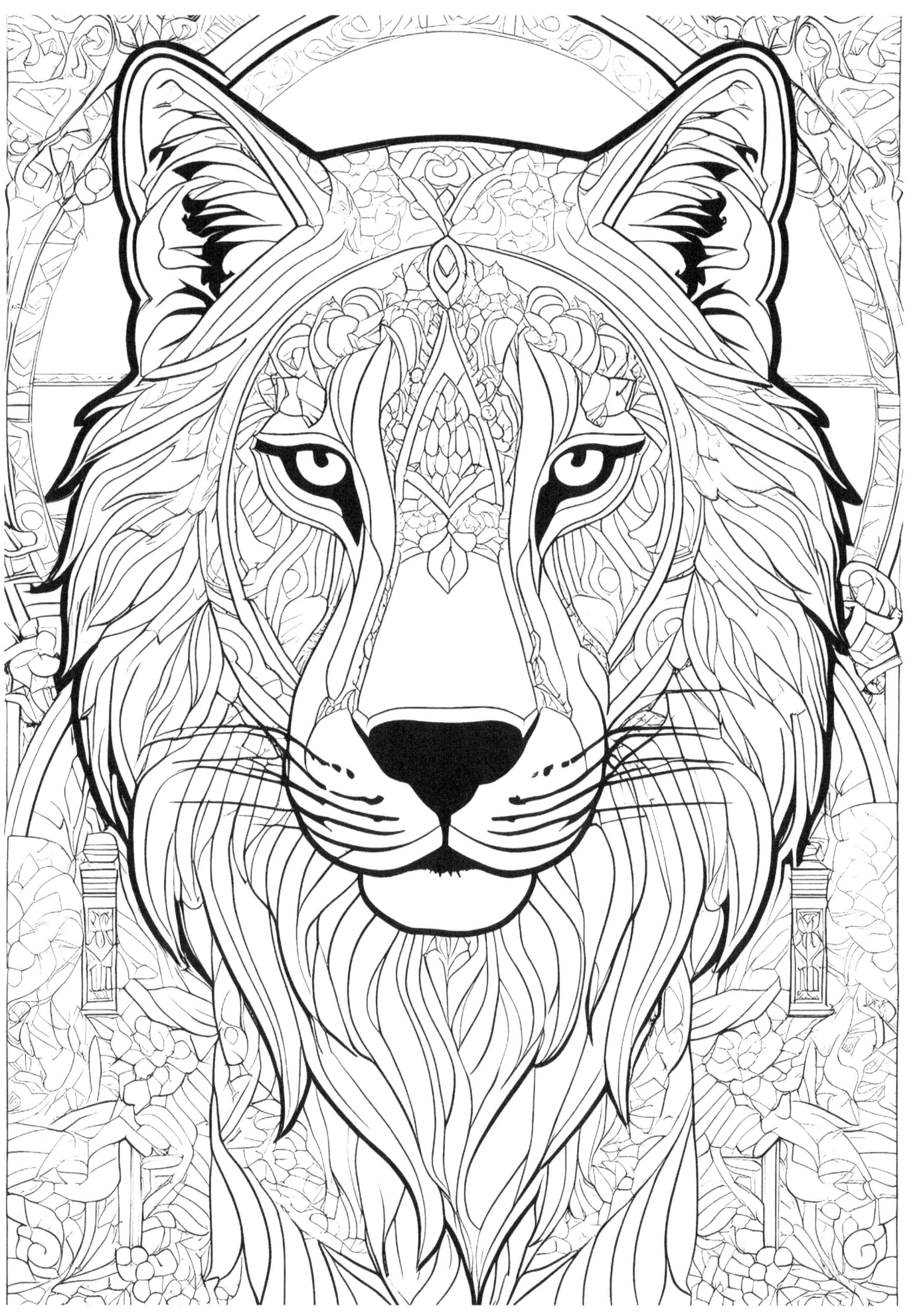

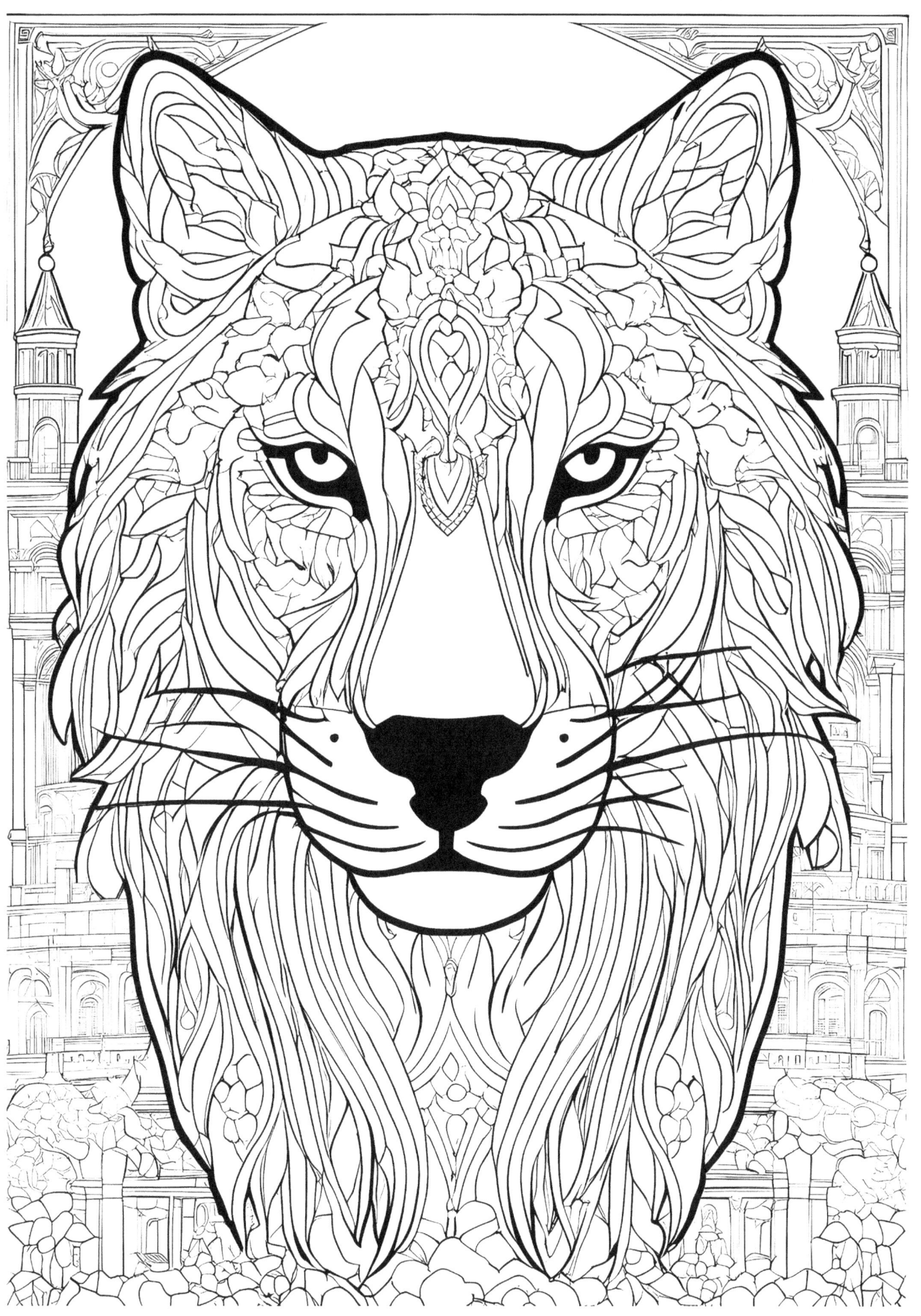

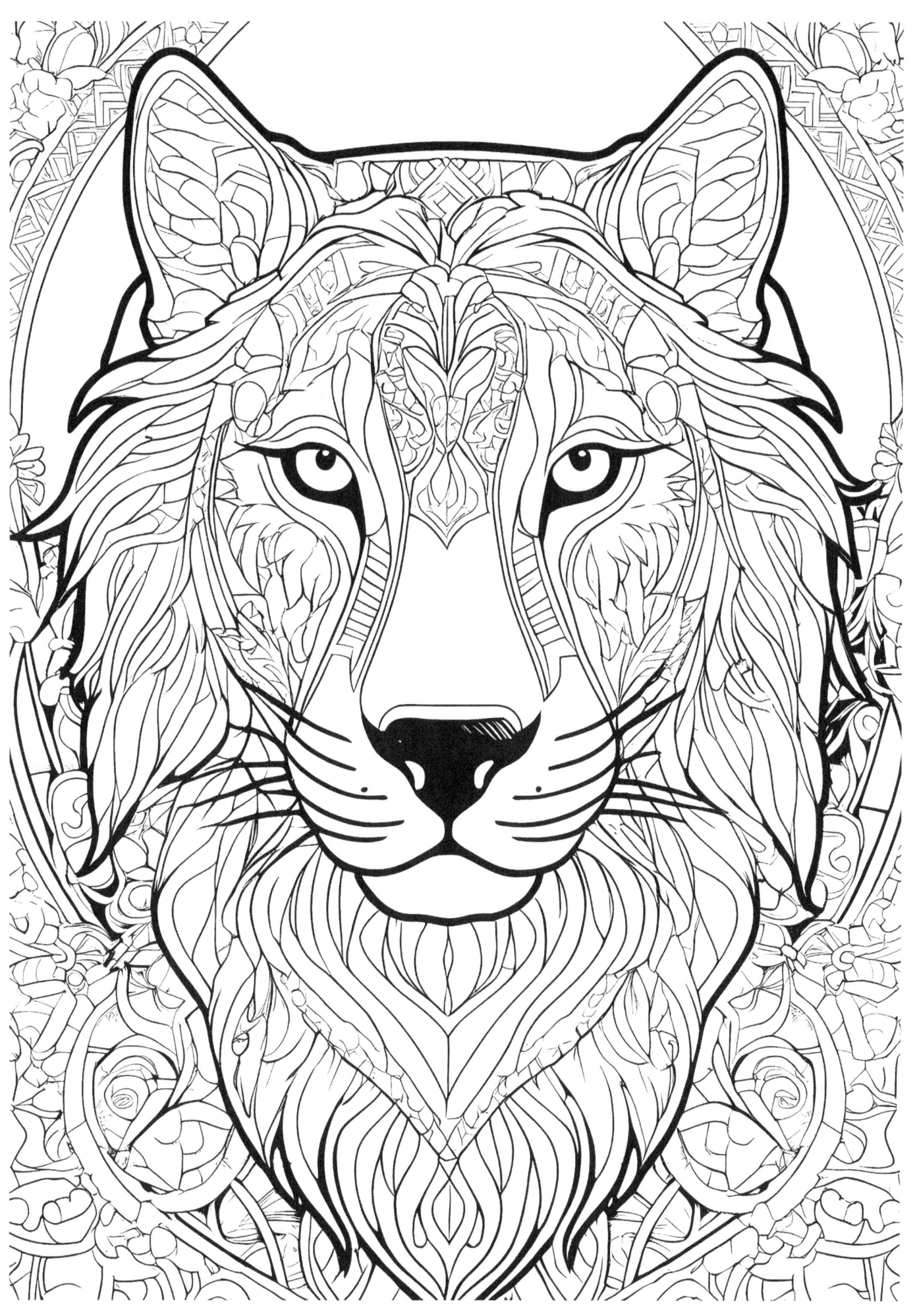

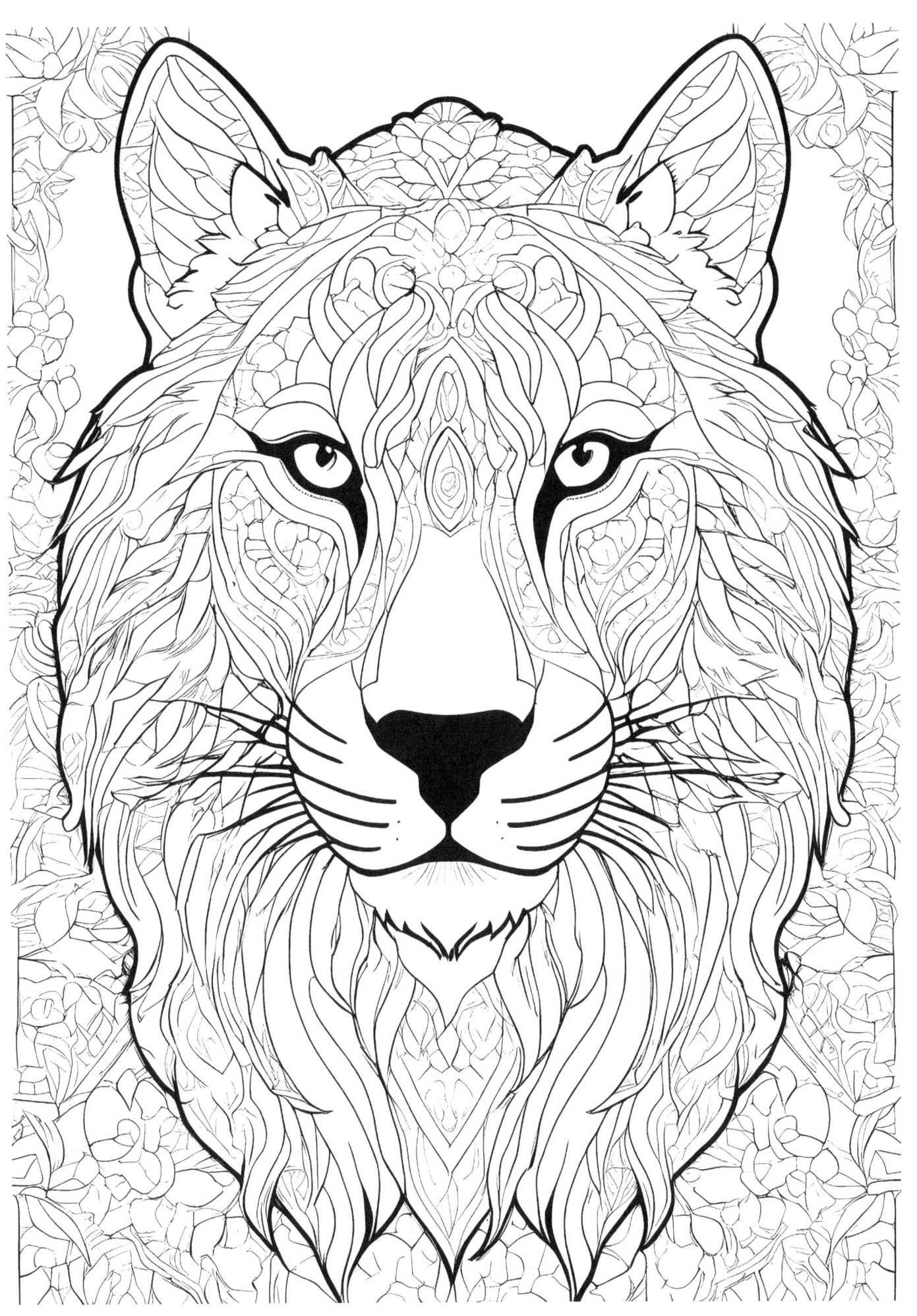

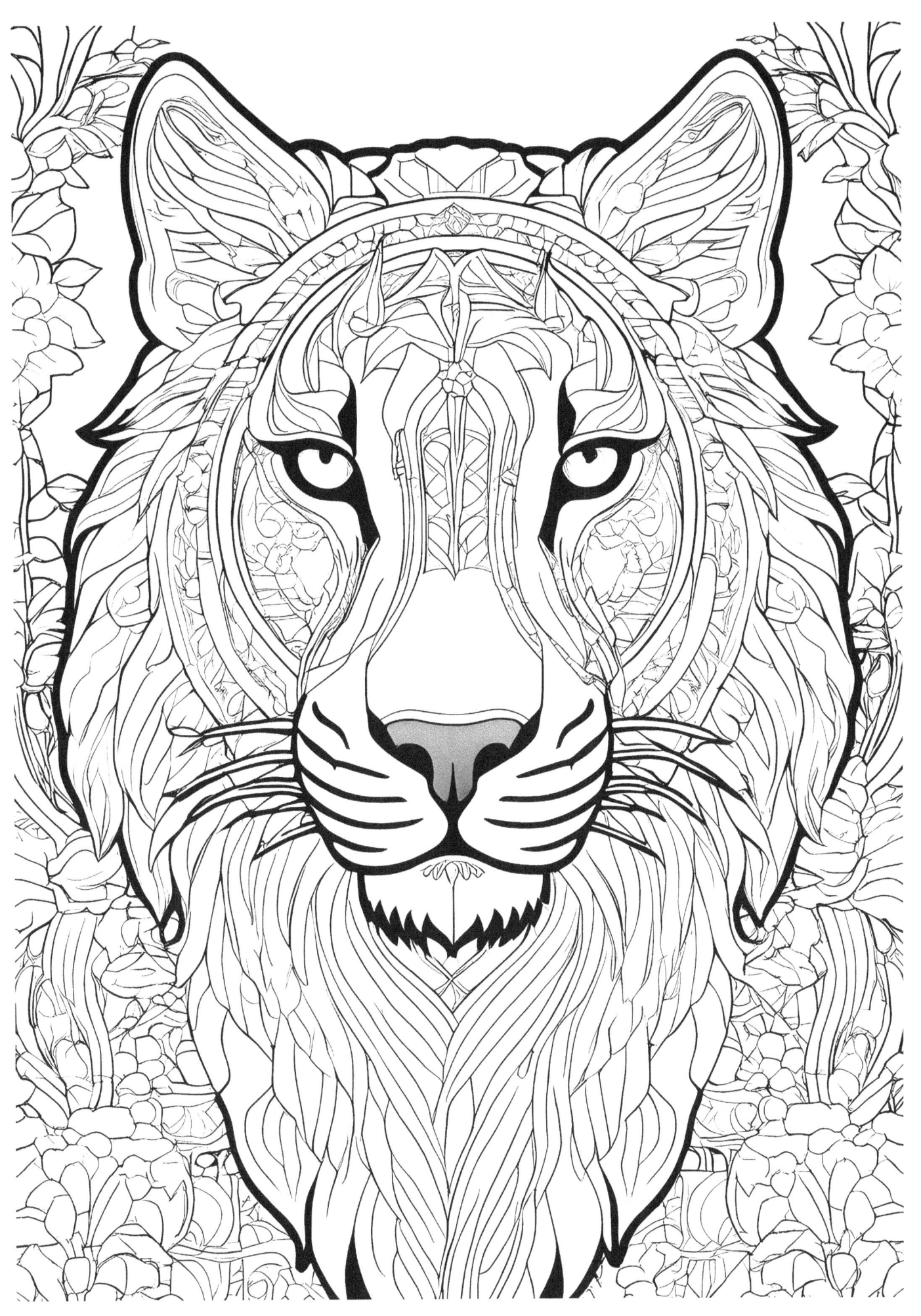

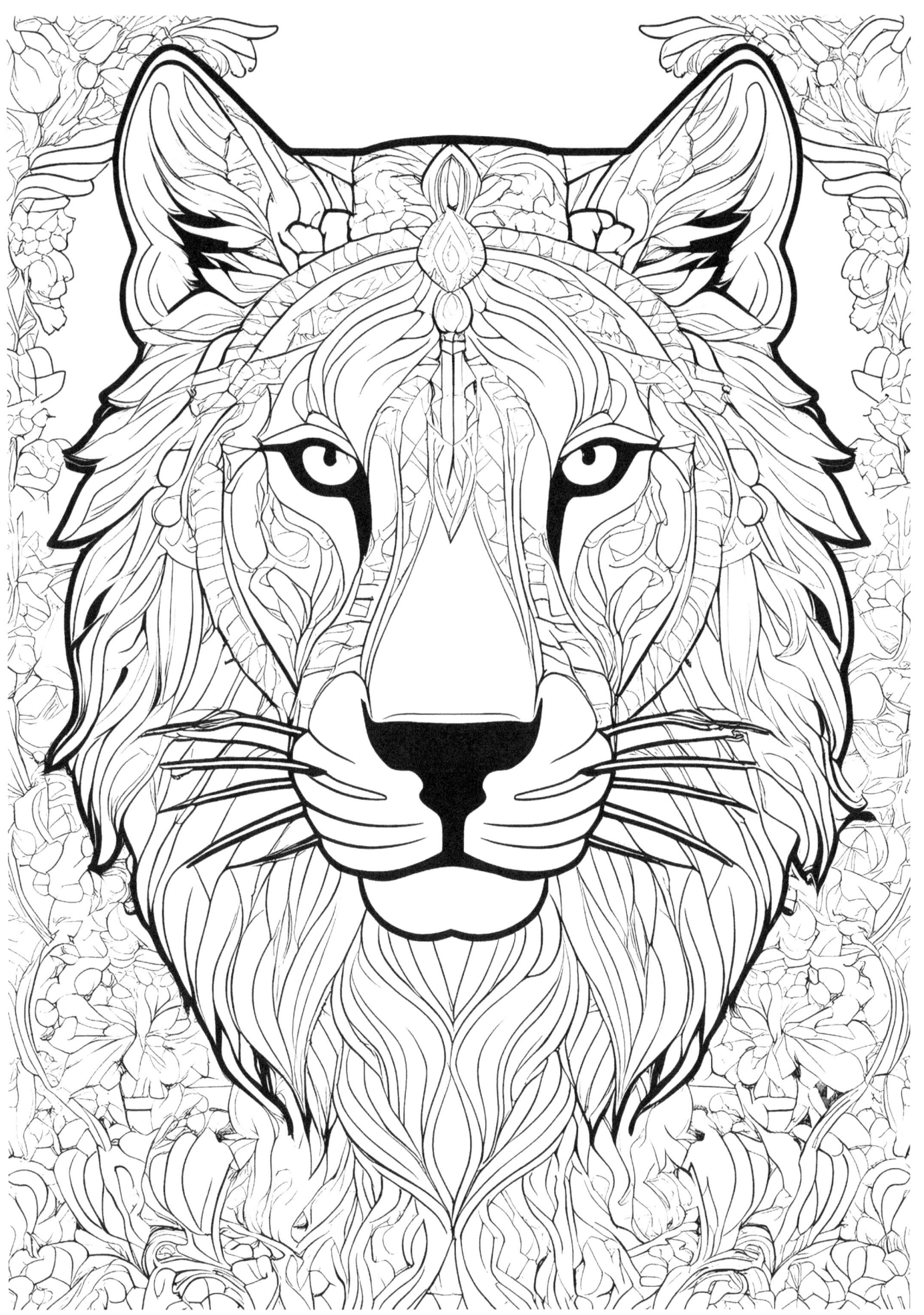

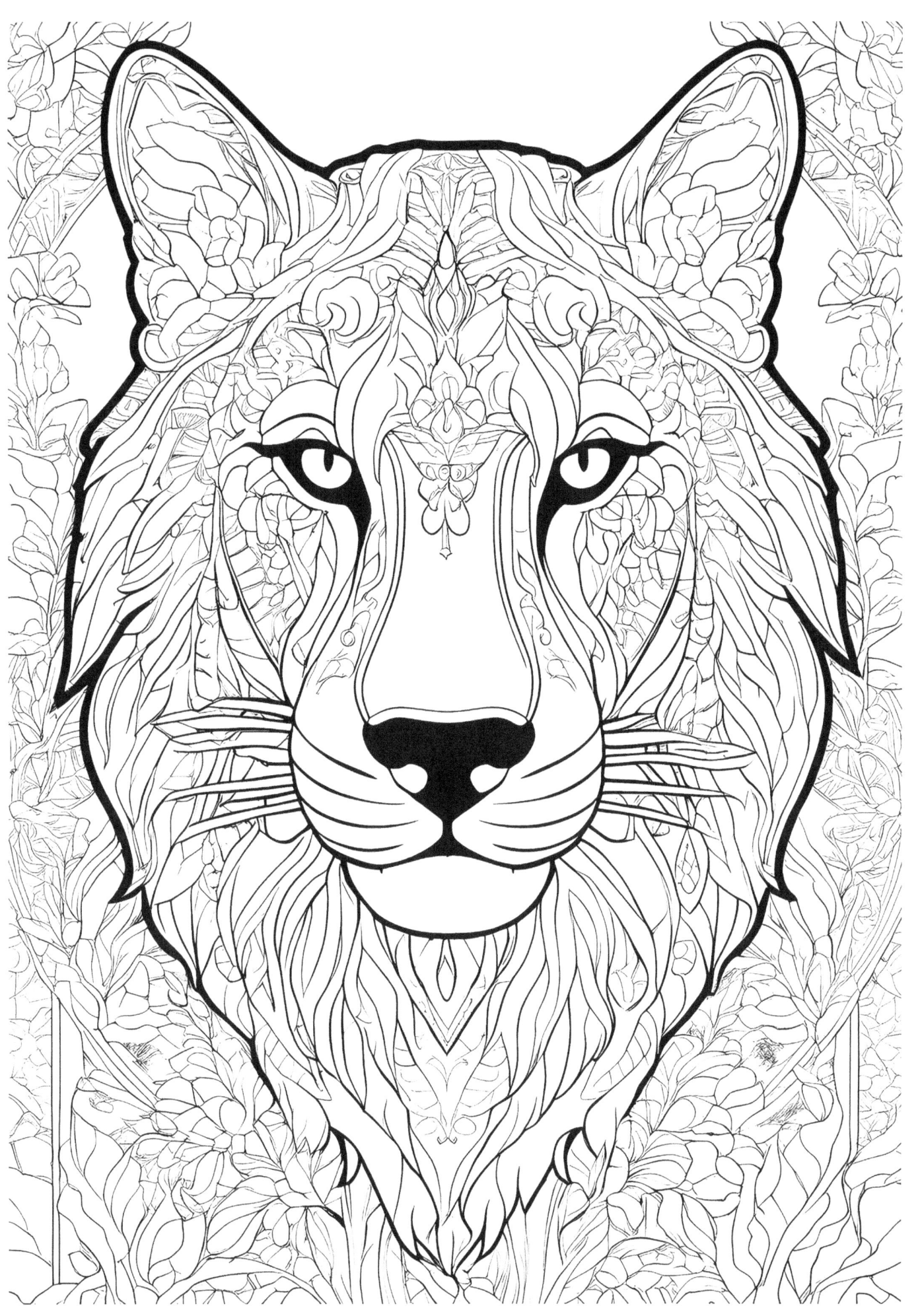

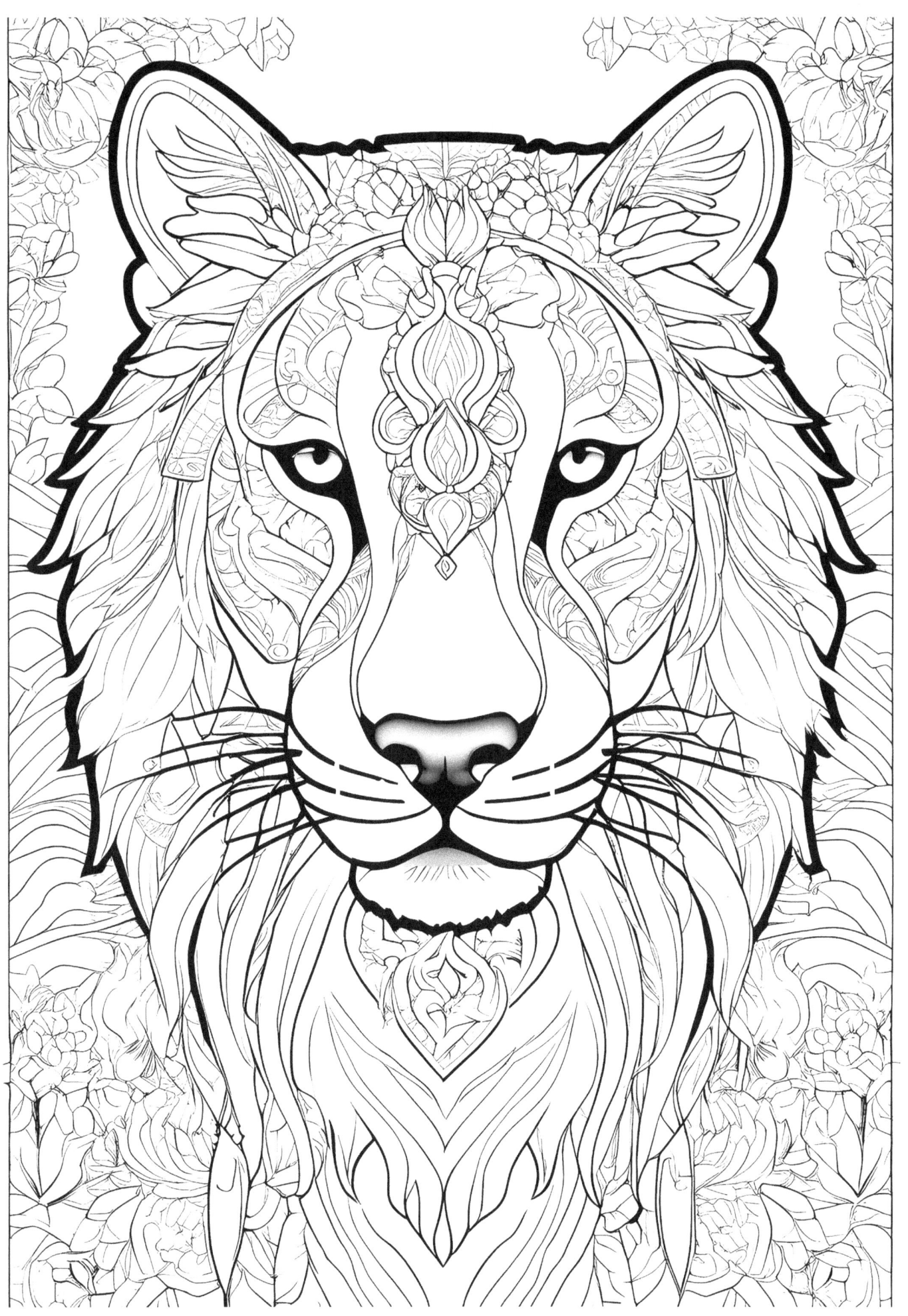

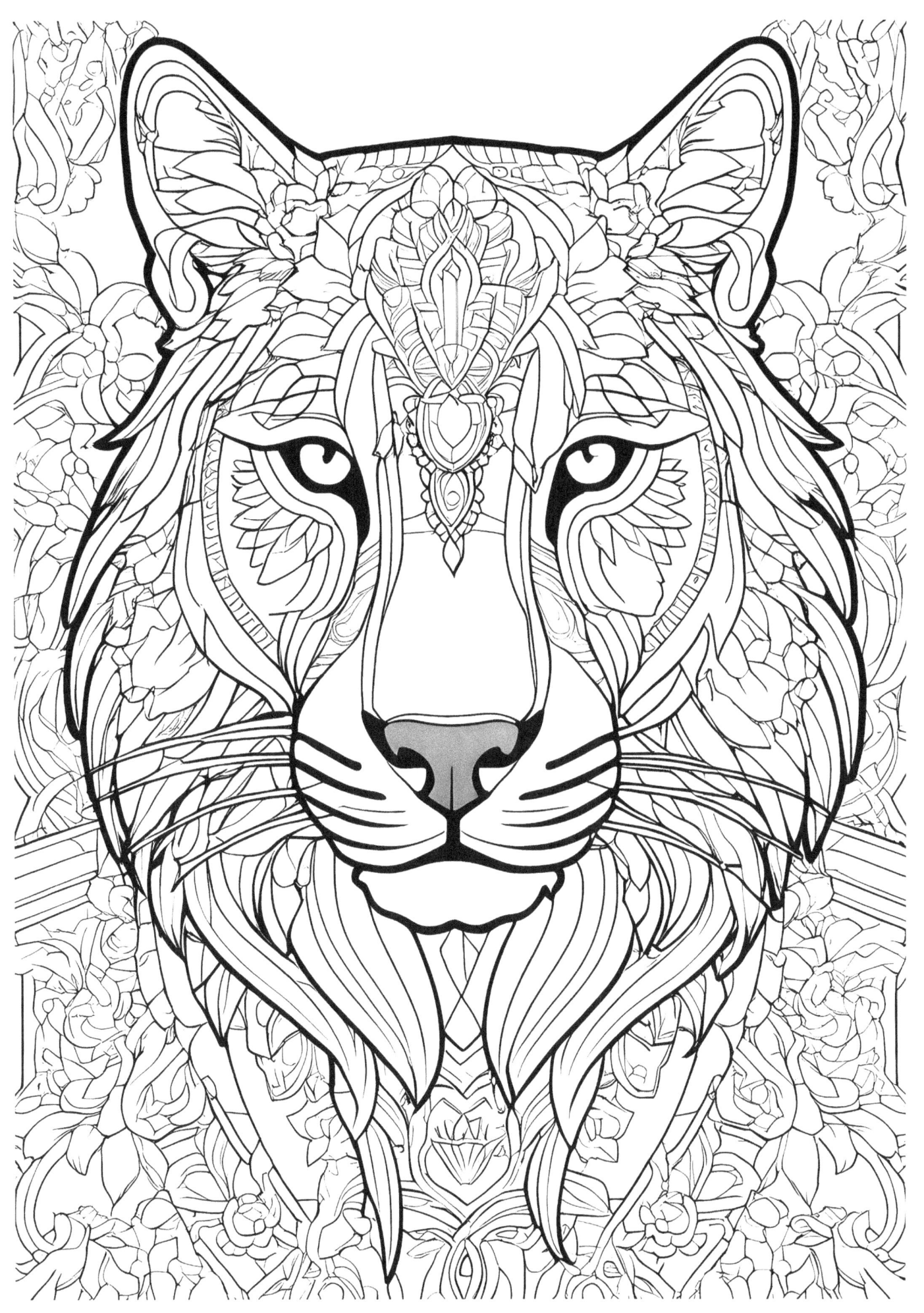

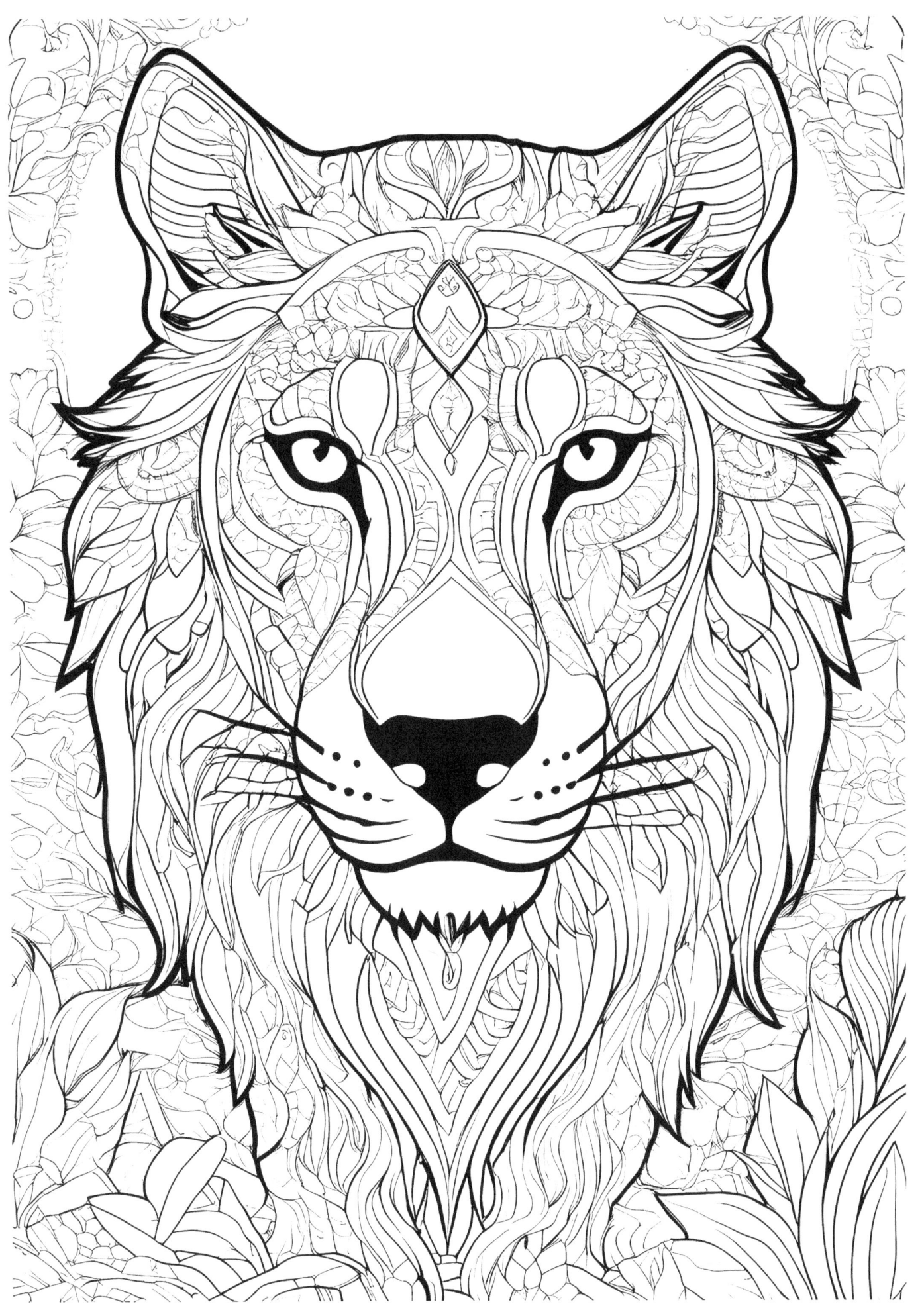

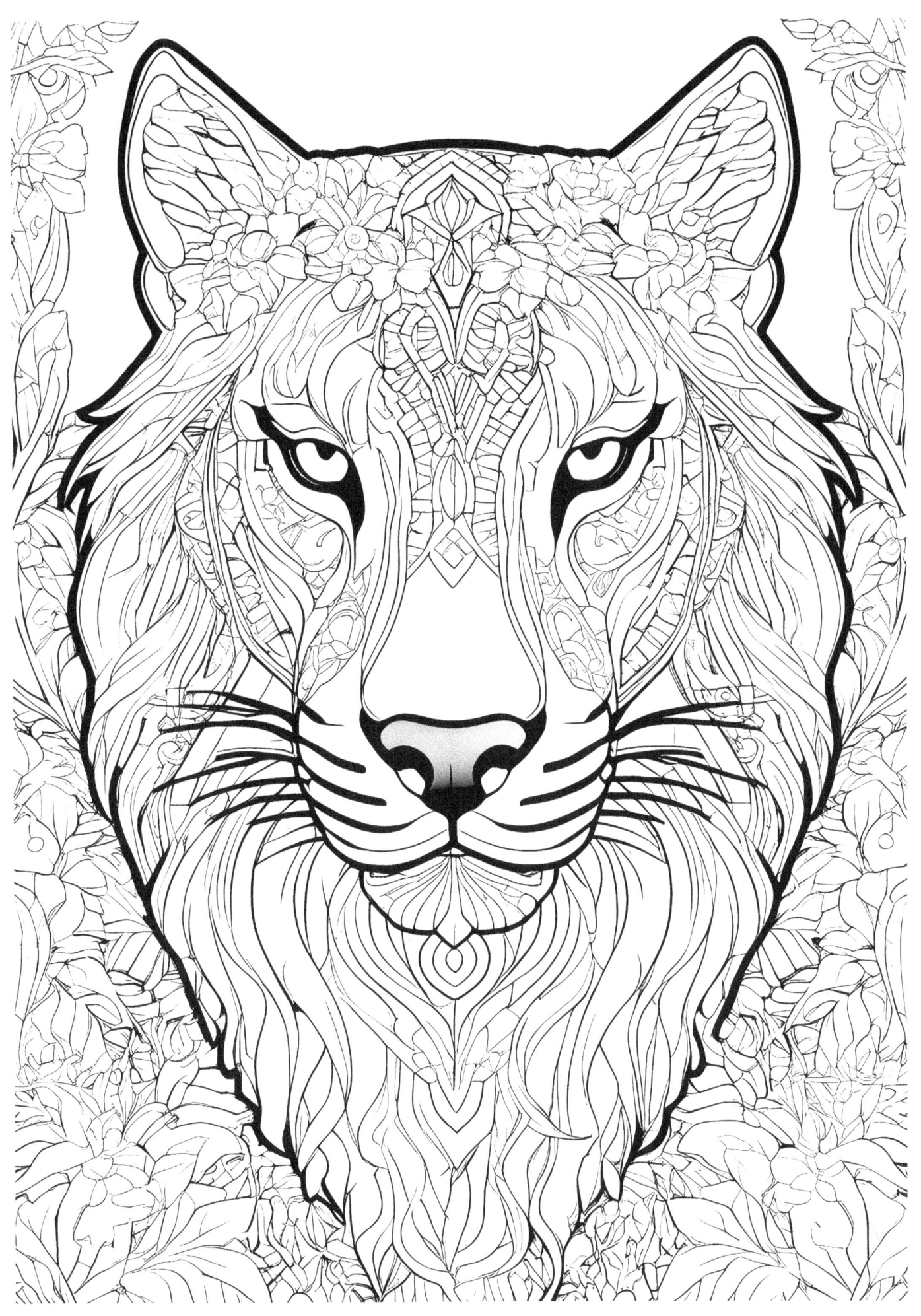

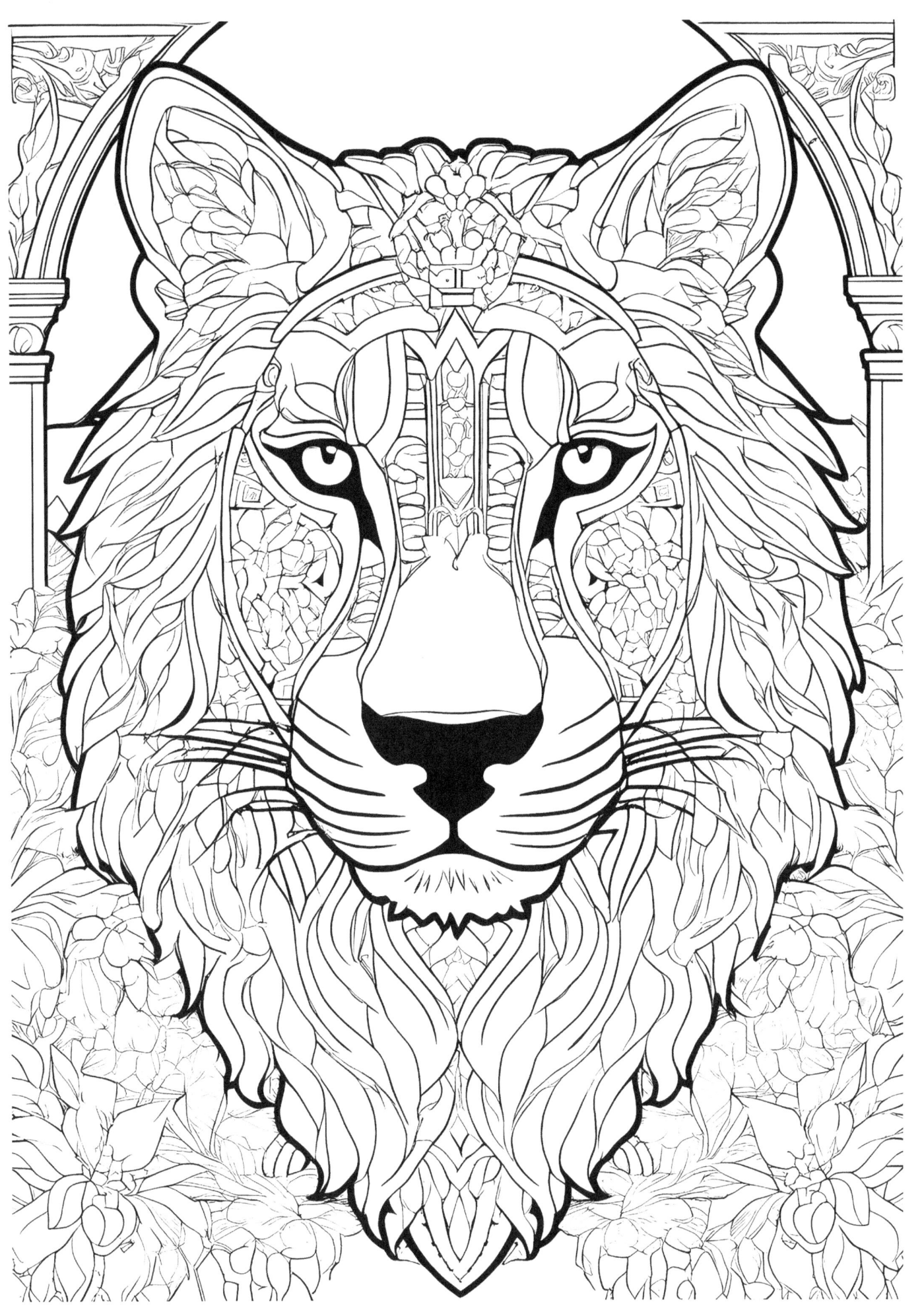

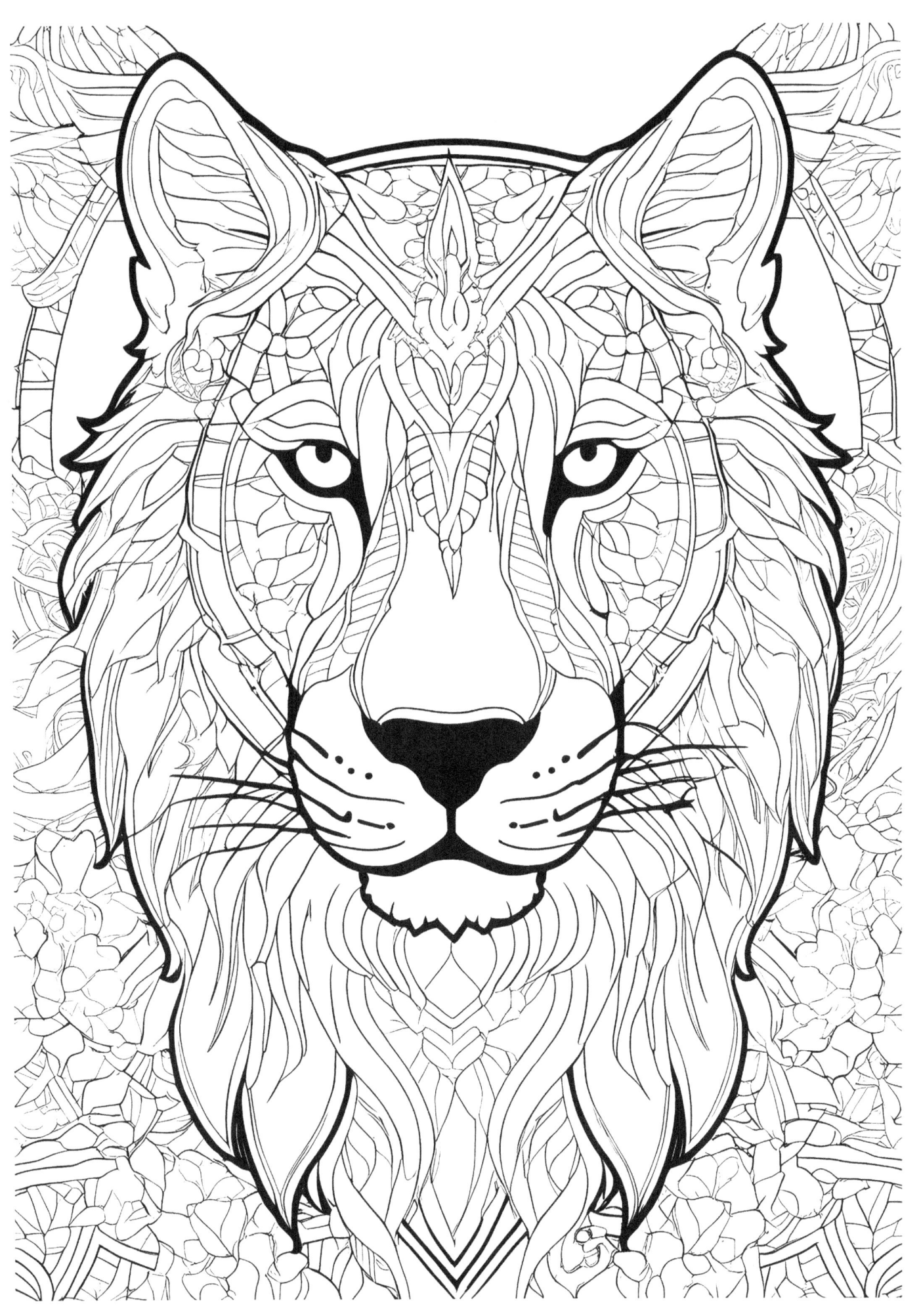

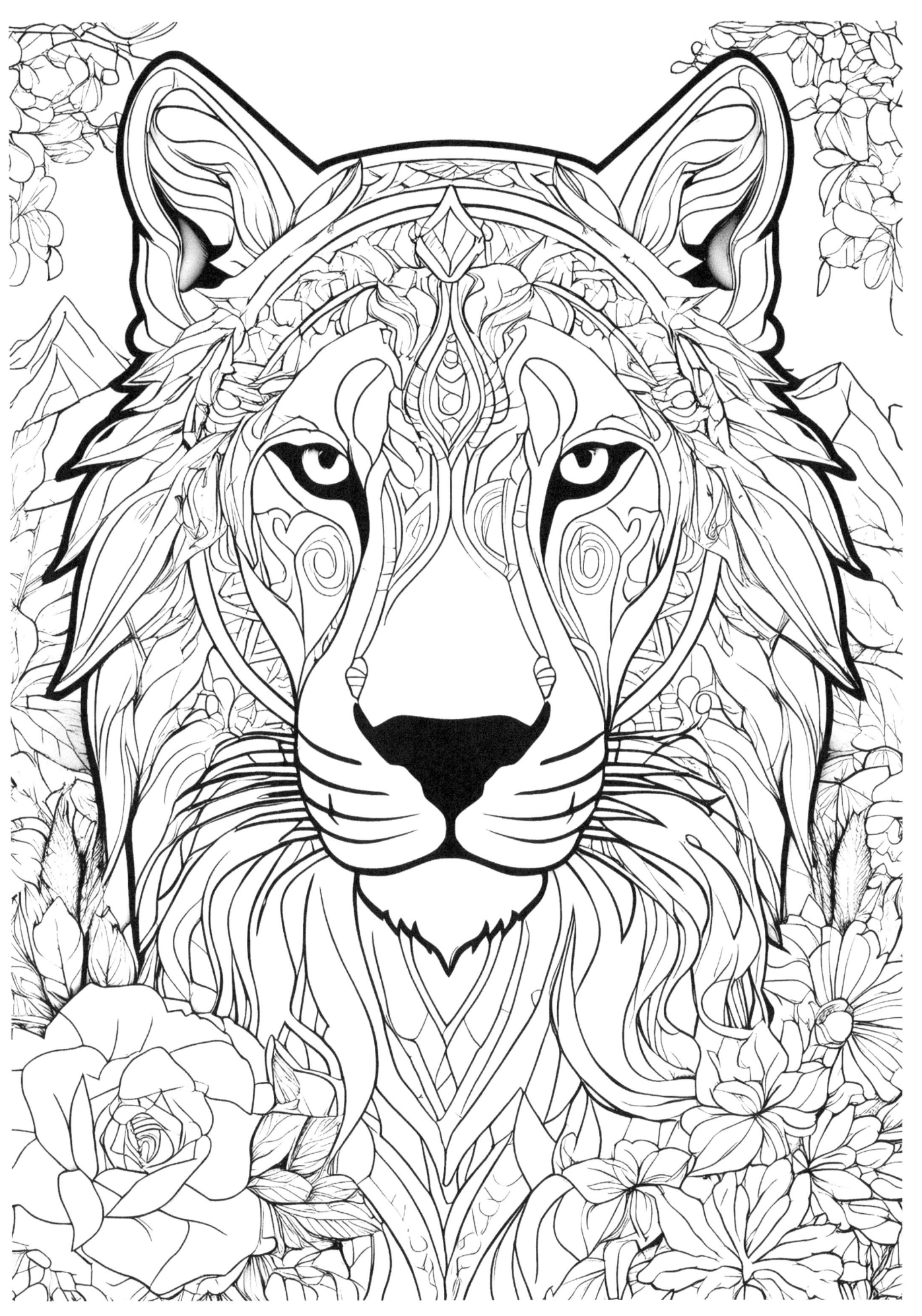

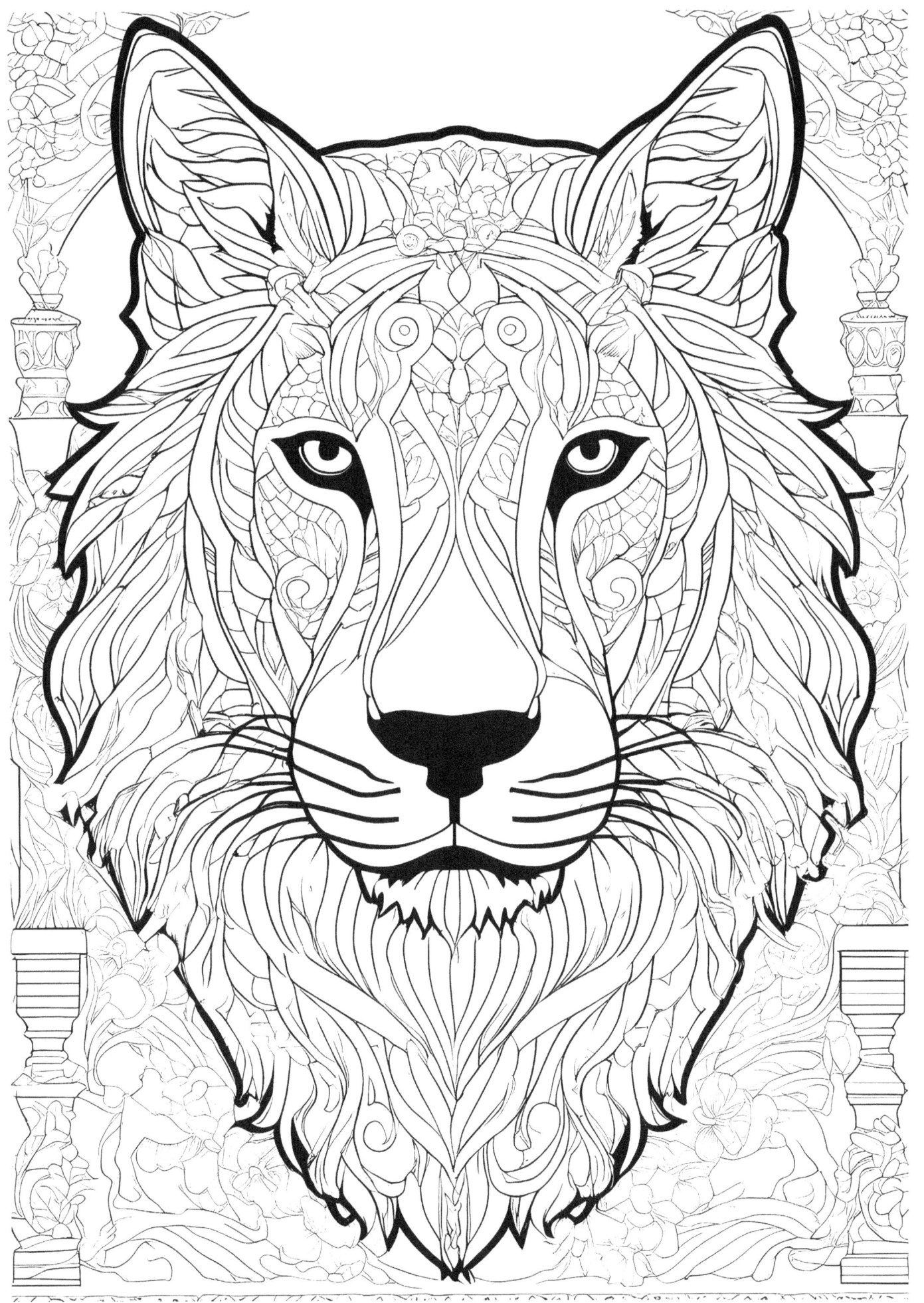

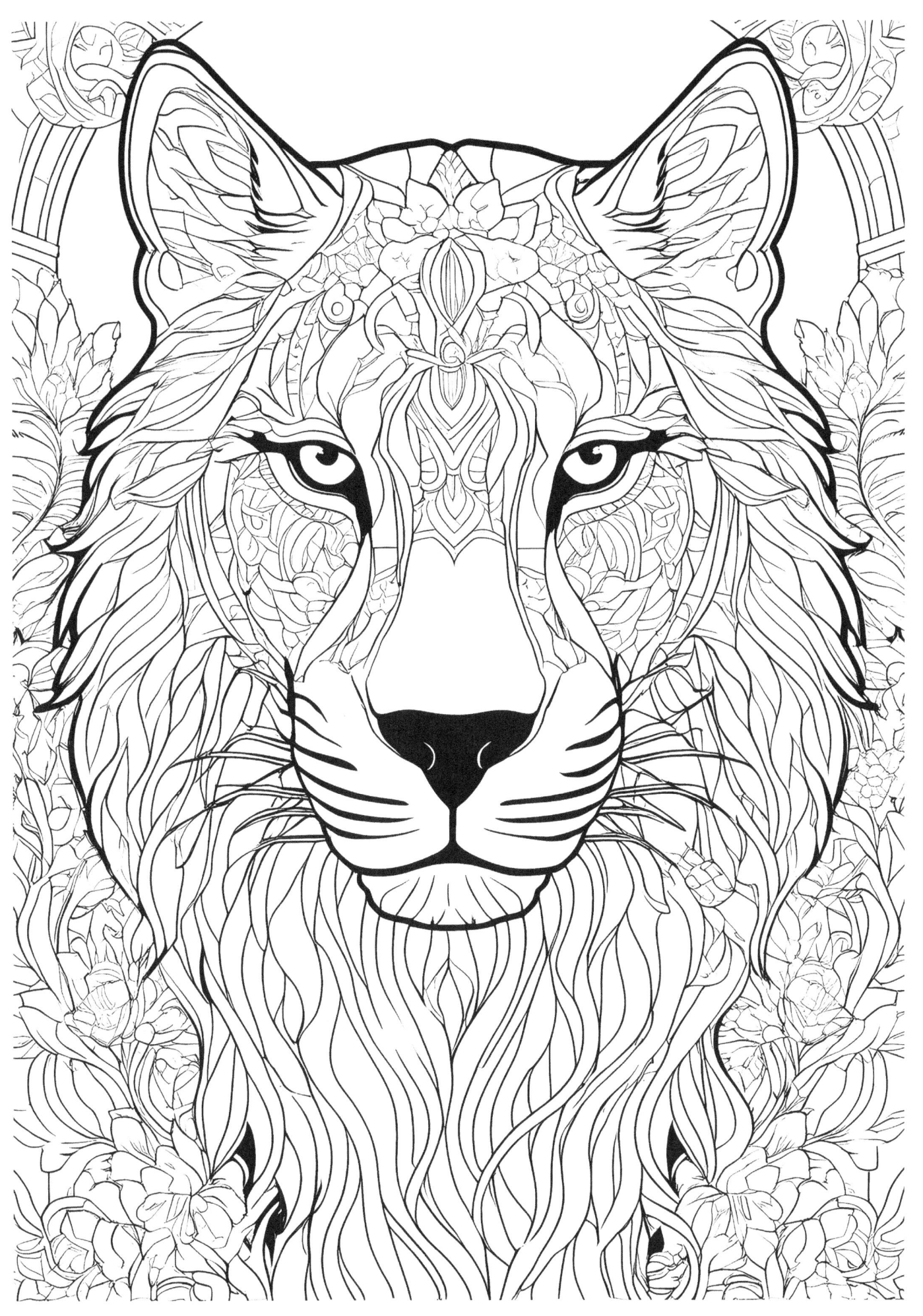

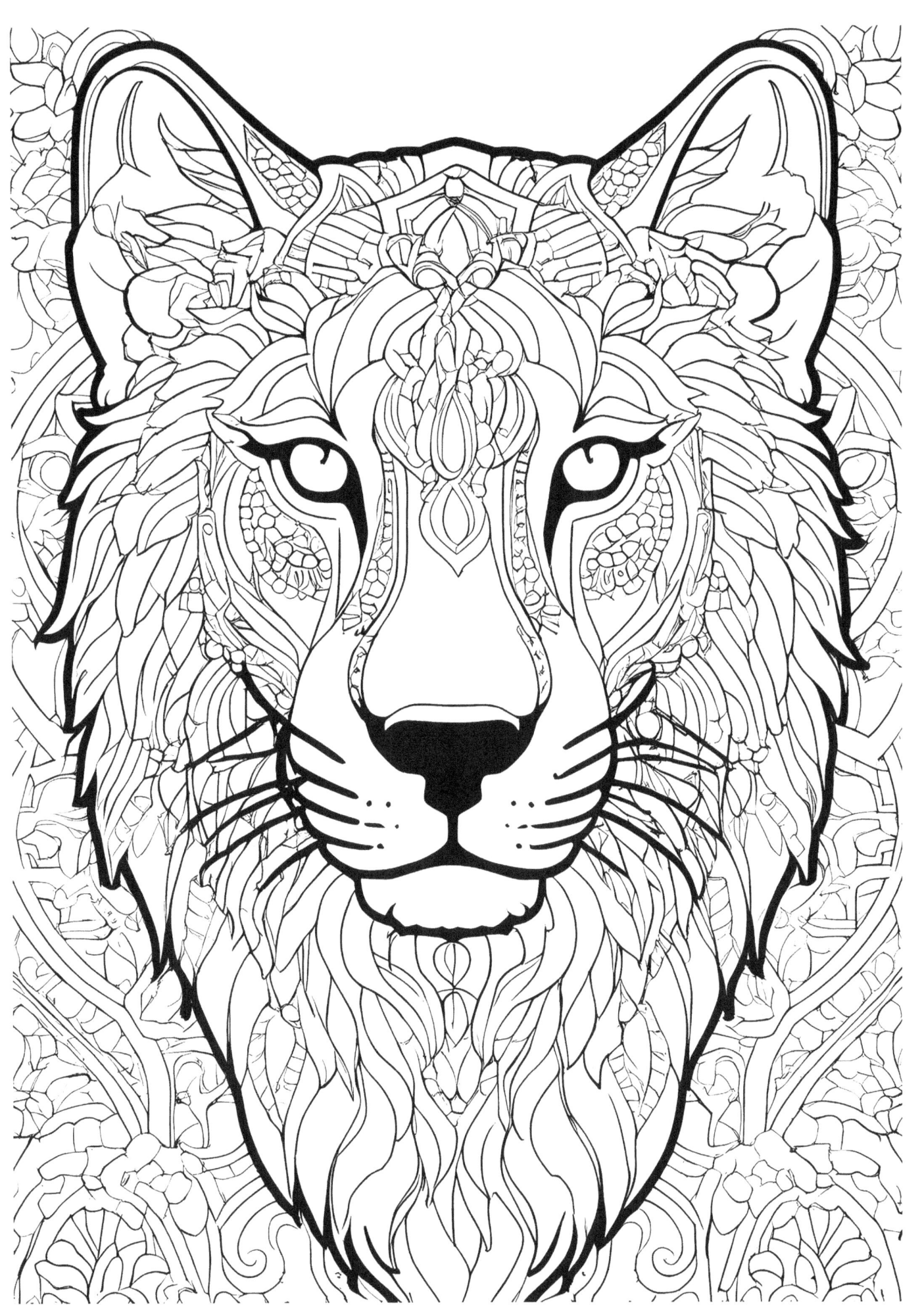

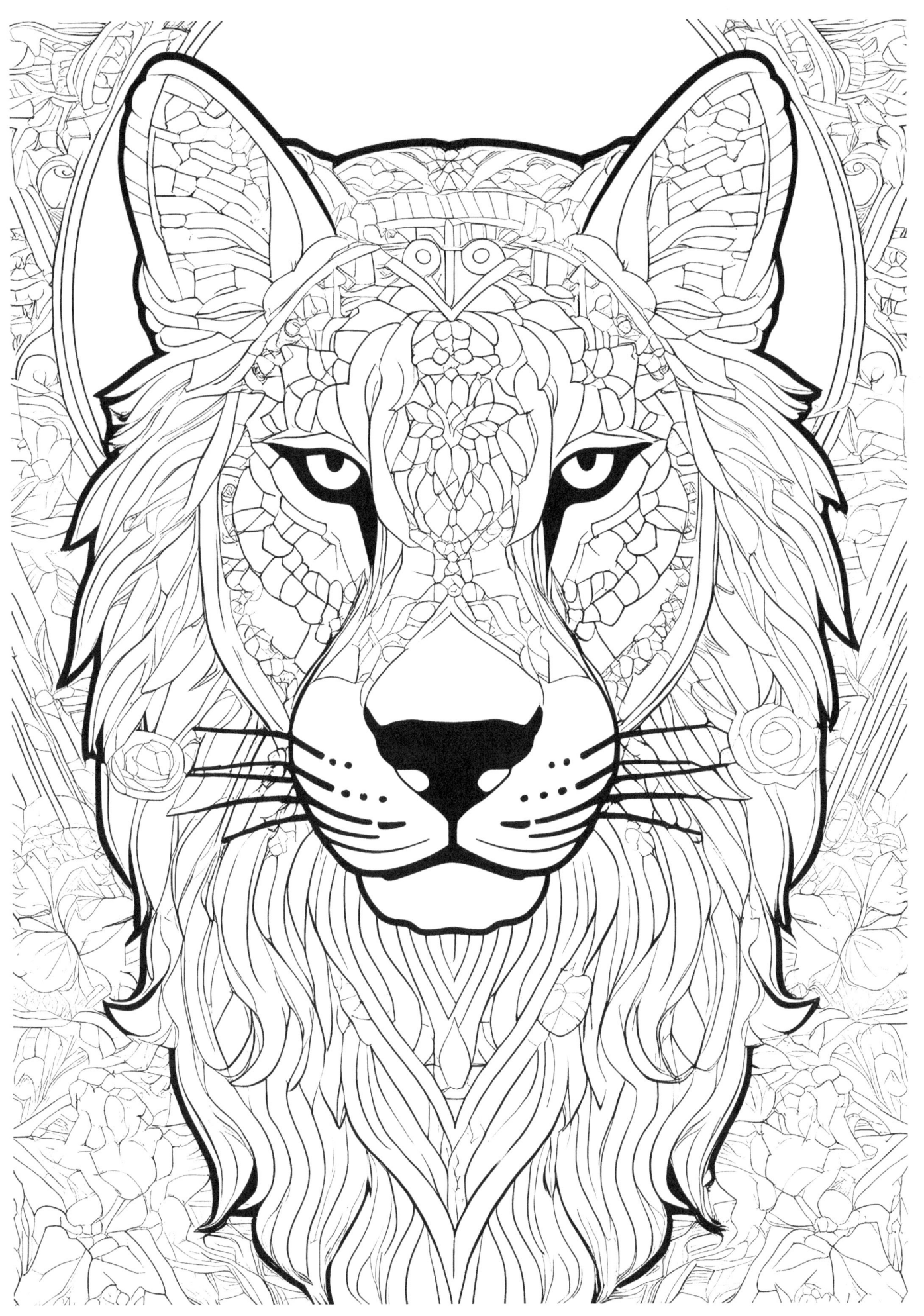

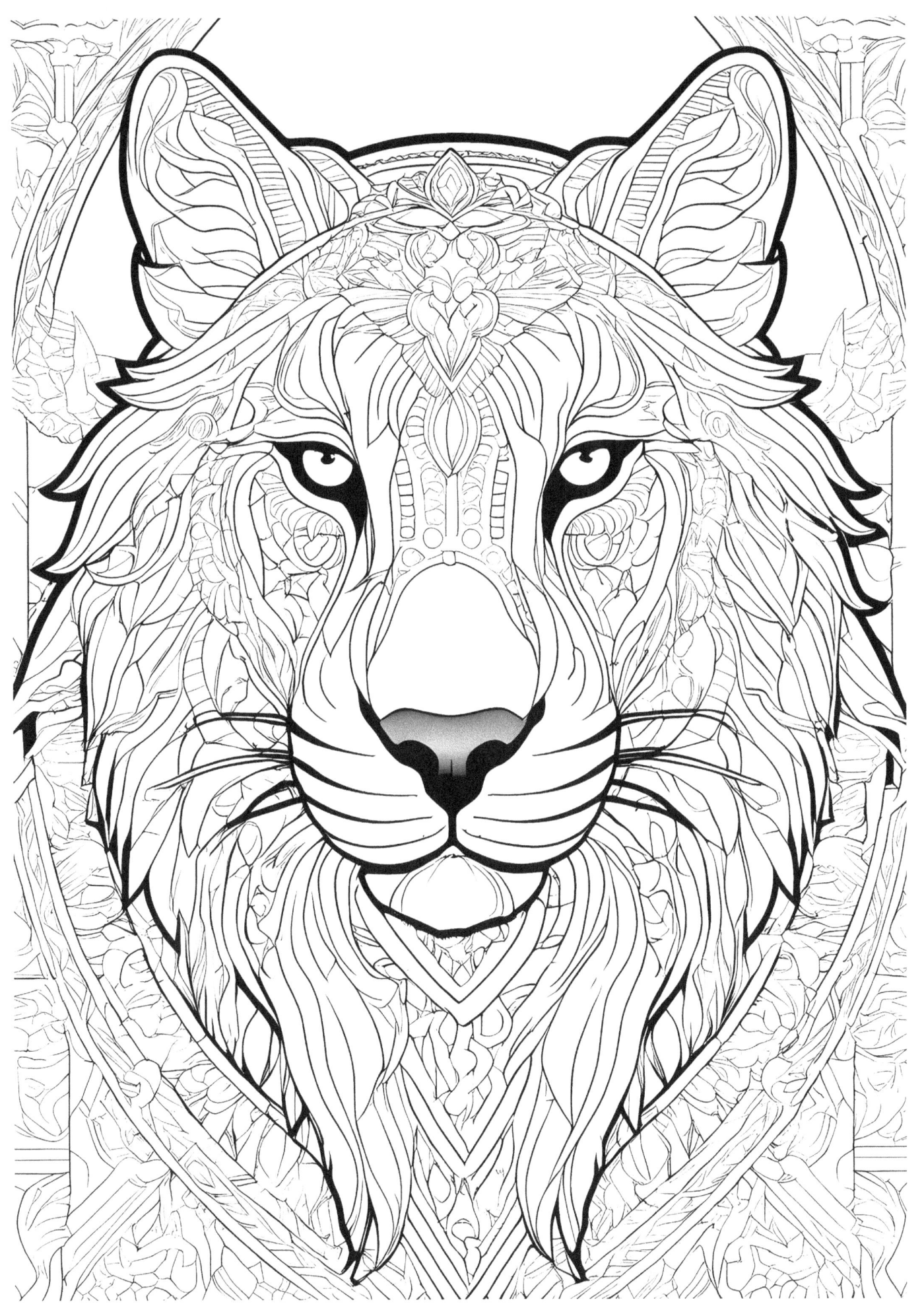

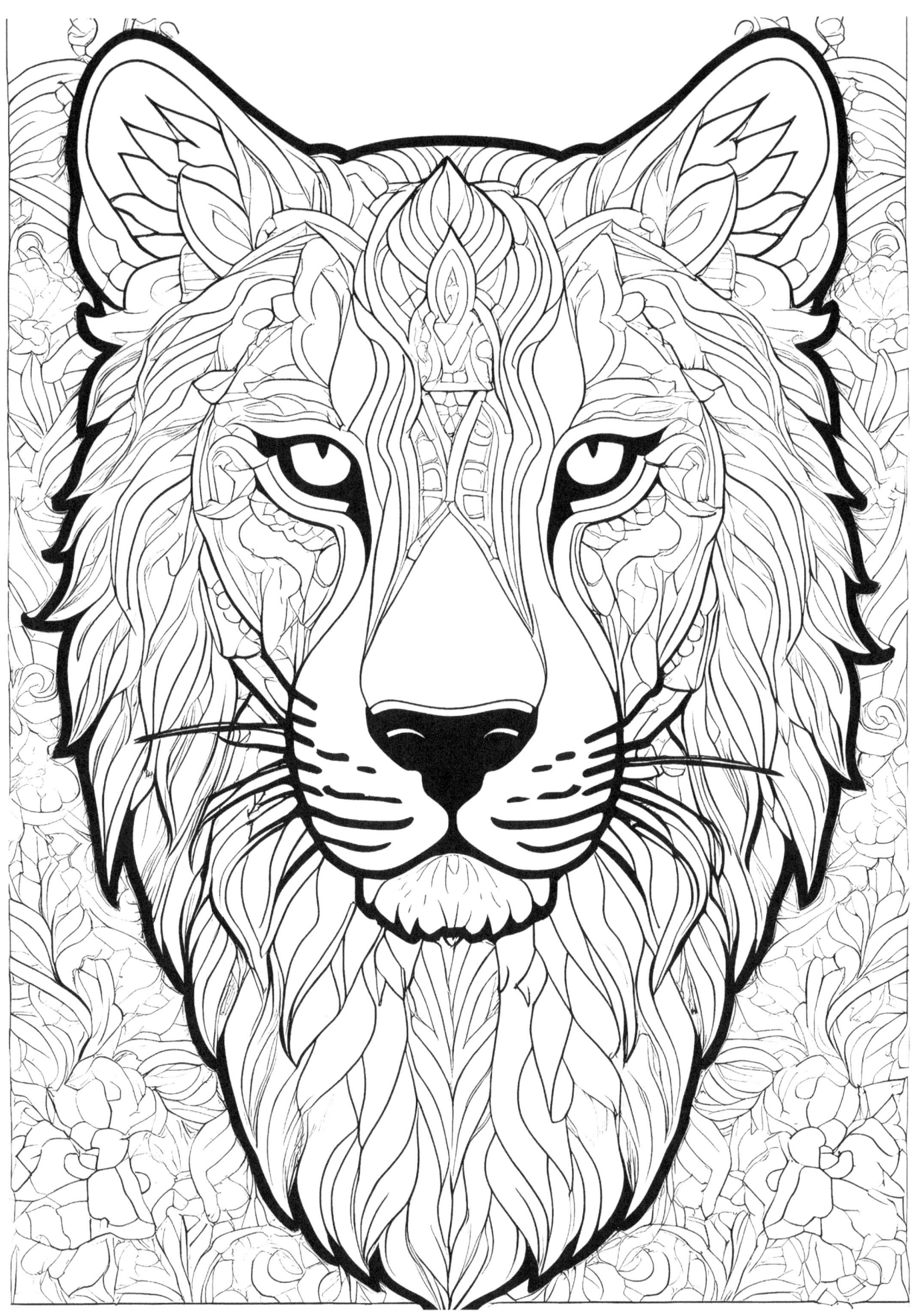

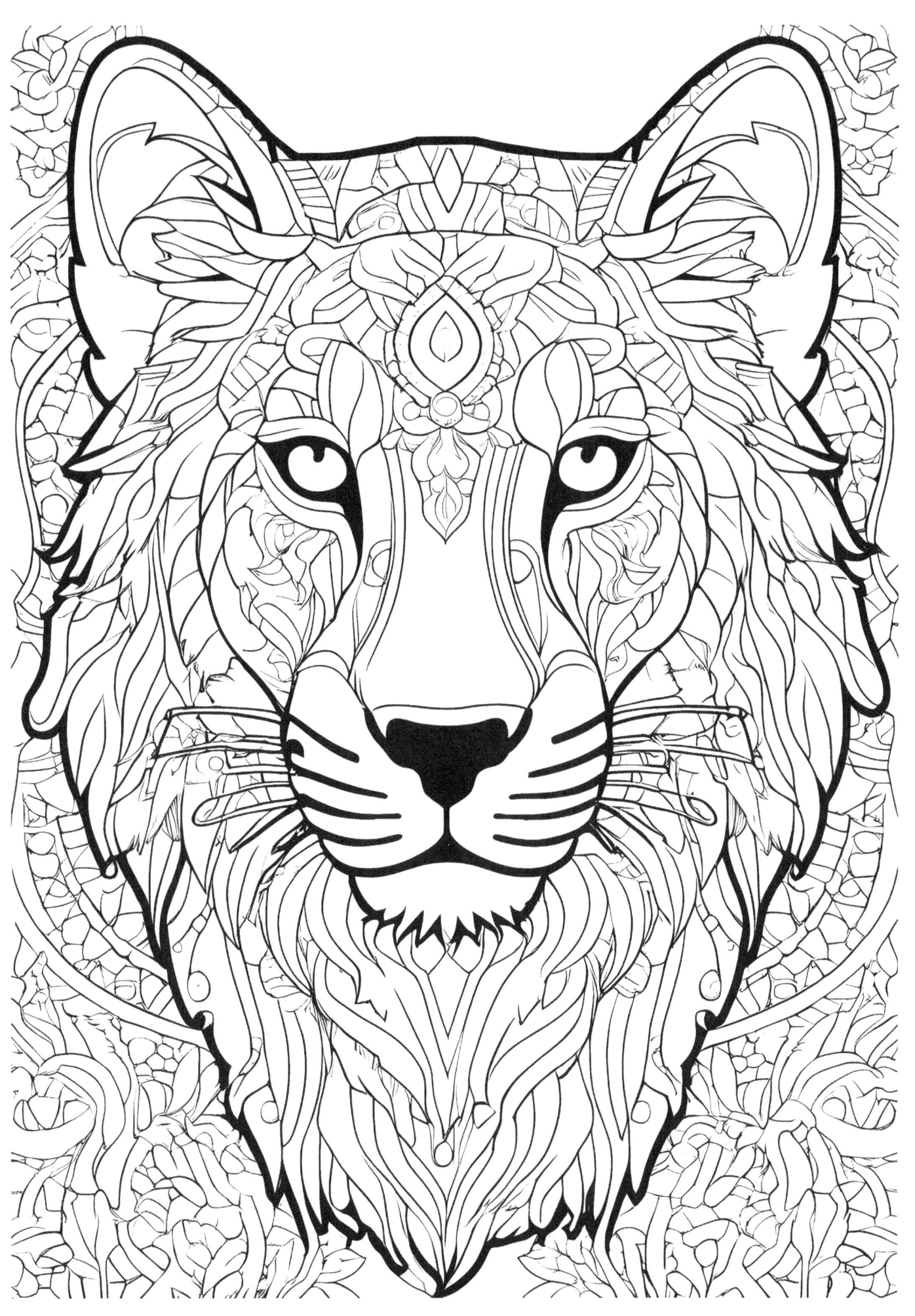

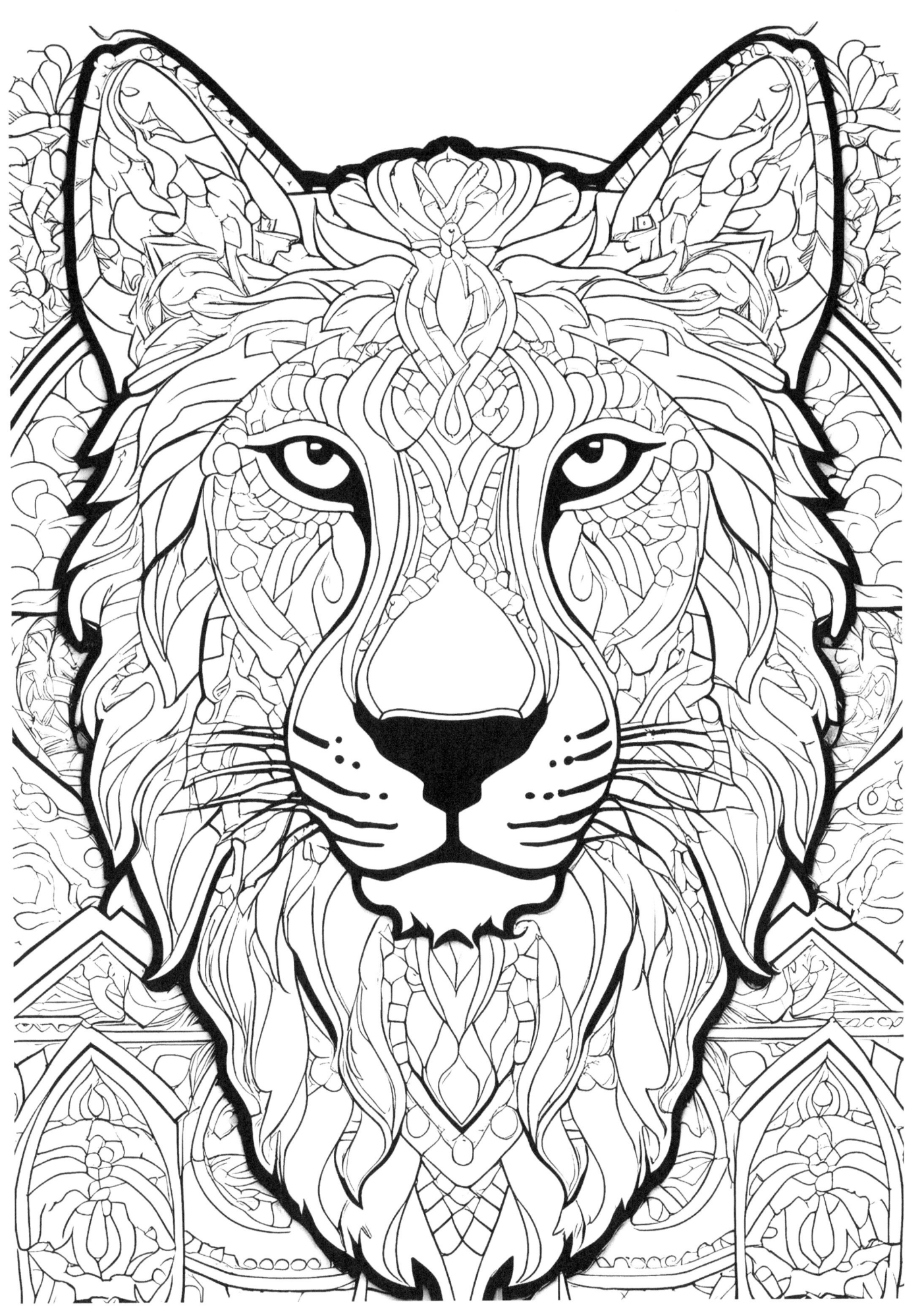

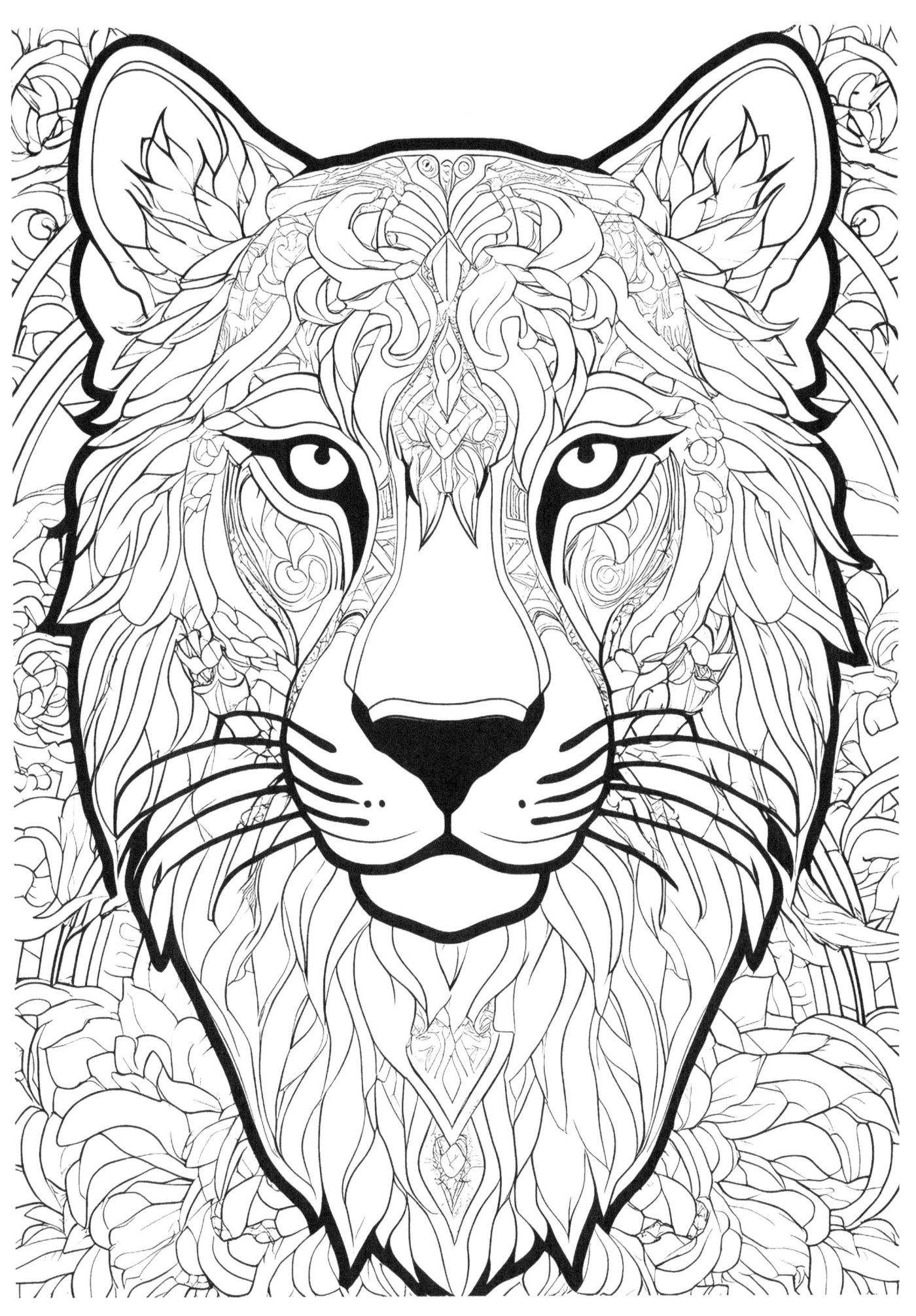

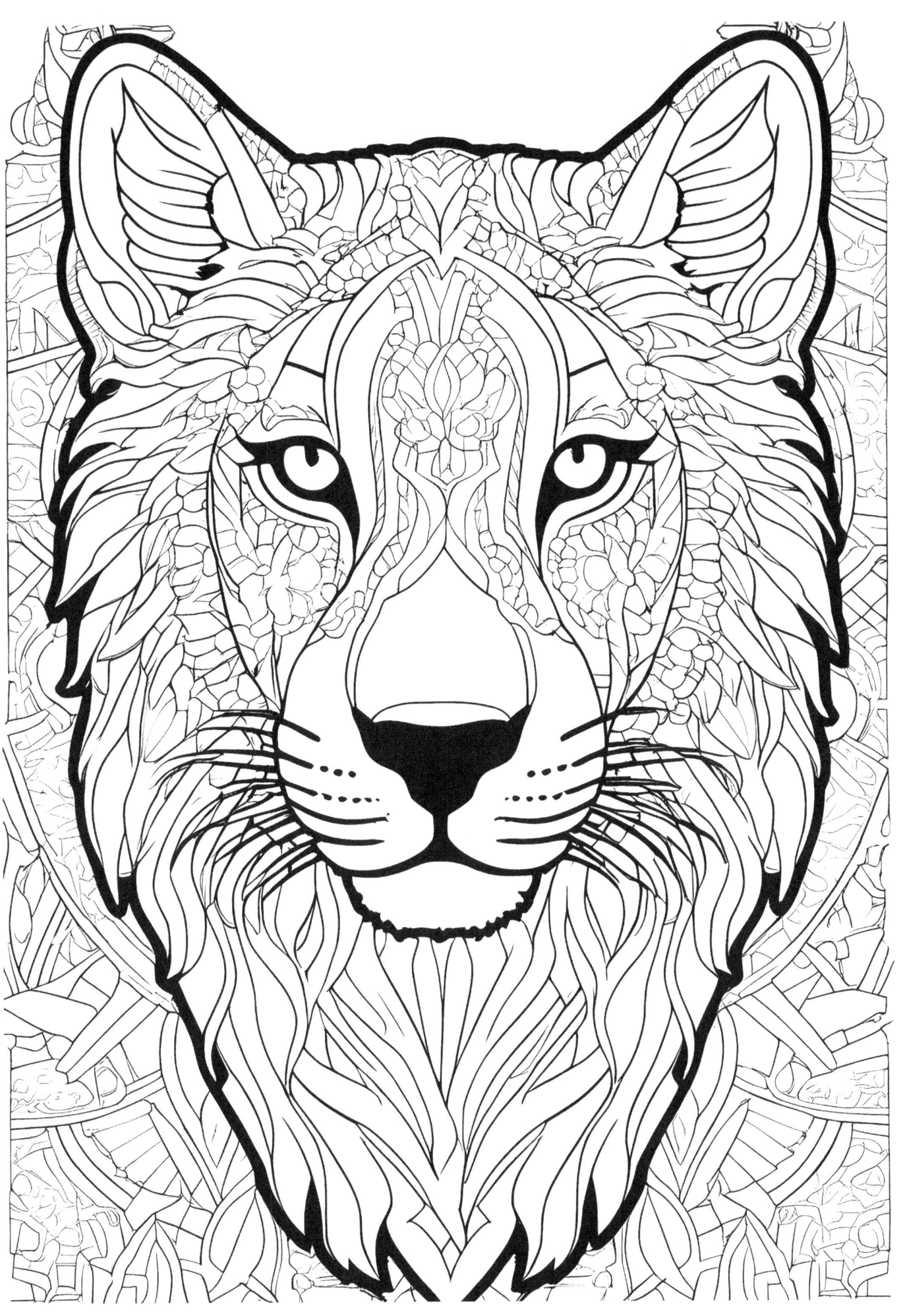

Remember that your creativity is a masterpiece. Keep coloring your world with imagination and curiosity. The adventure continues beyond these pages. Happy coloring, and may your days be filled with colorful wonders!